COACHING THE OFFENSIVE LINE:

BY THE EXPERTS

Edited by
Earl Browning

ISBN: 1-57167-425-x

Library of Congress Catalog Card Number: 99-62975

Cover Design: Jennie Scott

Front Cover Photo: Courtesy of the University of Kentucky

Developmental Editor: Kim Heusel

Page Layout: Kim Heusel

Coaches Choice Books is a division of:

Sagamore Publishing, Inc.

P.O. Box 647

Champaign, IL 61824-0647

Web Site: http://www.sagamorepub.com

Table of Contents

Chapter 1

UTILIZING THE TIGHT END

By
Greg Adkins
University of Georgia
1998

I am going to talk about the use of our tight end in our offense. We do a lot with our tight end. They are run blockers, pass receivers, and they are pass protectors. This past year we were in a tight-end set for 190 snaps. That comes out to one-sixth of the time we were in a tight-end set.

First I want to talk about our practice schedule. Our ends are involved in a great deal of our practice. This is a general practice that we would go through with our tight ends.

PRACTICE SCHEDULE

Period

1-5	Individual Ball Drills
	Board and Chutes
	Angle Boards
	Combos with Tackles
	Running Game Assignment
6-7	Inside Drill and 1 on 1 vs. Defensive Back
8-10	Team Pass
11-13	Skelly
14-22	Team Work
23-24	Special Teams

The first five periods are our Individual Drills. The first thing we do is to catch some footballs. Then we do different ball drills. We go down with the offensive line and go through some board drills and work on our basic steps. Then we go to the Angle Boards and work on our Down Blocks. Next we do our Combo Blocks with our Tackles. We are basically a Zone Blocking Team. Then we do some Running Game Assignments with our offensive line while we are there. We are in this session about 10 minutes.

Next we go to our Inside Drills and our 1 on 1 vs. Defensive Backs. I have four ends and I send a couple of them to work one on one with the defensive backs. I will rotate them around. Two will work on the inside drill and two will work on the one-on-one drills.

Next we go to our Team Passing Drills. This is our 1's against 1's. We do this two days per week during the season. We go for eight plays. The defense can do whatever it wants. This is an all-pass drill, and it is one of the best things we do. The offensive and defensive lines come off the ball and work on their skills.

Next is our Skelly Drill vs. Defensive Backs. We spend 20 to 25 minutes on this drill.

Our next session is our Team Work. The time varies on this area, depending on the day.

Our last period is with our Special Teams. Tight ends are usually good athletes and they are involved on special teams as most of ours are.

The next thing I want to talk about is the Motion Game that we use. We try to create some mismatches by using motion. We set the formation and motion the end over across the formation and bring him back. We jet him across and create a trips formation. We bring him back and run the toss sweep to that side. We like to put the tight ends side by side.

The next thing we will do is to have two tight ends in their normal position and have two wide receivers to one side.

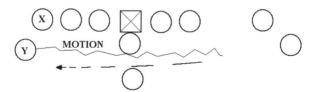

The other formation we like to use is with two tight ends and two receivers. We have a tight end and wide receiver on each side. We can line up that way or have the end move to that set.

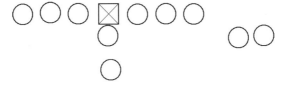

We will start with both tight ends on the line. Then we move one of them back off the line and motion him across the formation. When we do that we can create a wing formation. We give them several different things out of that set. We can run the Toss Sweep to the two tight ends, and we can Counter Trey back away where we pull the two guards.

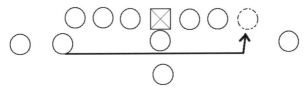

We can run our Combination Routes with the two receivers on each side as well. You can run any pattern you want.

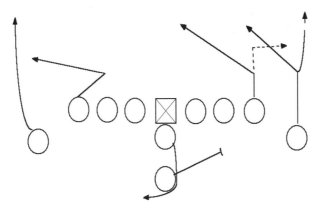

We do use other formations where we only use one tight end in the game. We run the basic trips set that everyone uses. When we run this formation we are trying to get some kicked-over coverage. We like to put a good receiver on the split-end side to get a one-on-one situation. We get the same situation when we go to the trips set and create a tight end on the back side. We get a lot of kicked-over coverage against the second set.

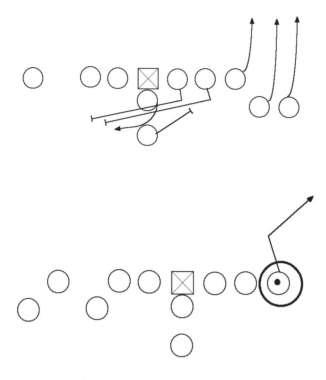

This is a formation we like a lot. We have two backs deep and we line the end up on the wing. We can bring him in motion and run the Toss Sweep and seal the inside. This has been a good formation for us.

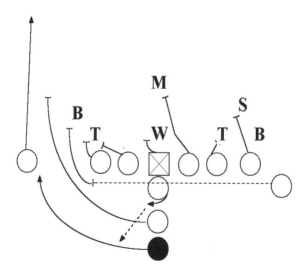

Next I want to talk about the running game we use with the two tight ends in the game. When we put the tight end in motion, the defense will kick over and try to stop the sweep to that side. We come back and run the inside zone play to the other side. We combo block the Mike and run inside.

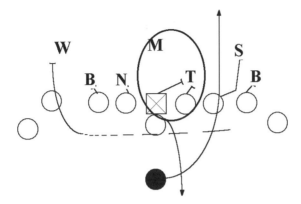

In the next formation most teams will try to balance against this. Again, the Inside Zone play is very simple. We work together with the tackle and end, and the center and the guard. It is Zone Blocking. We cut the back-side guard off and put the tackle on Sam. If the Safeties are playing outside we can break the play for a long gain.

Against teams that like to kick the defense over we run the Counter Trey back to the other side as our power play. We call it our power play. We block down on the Mike and the nose. We pull the back-side guard and tackle and hit the play back over the tackle.

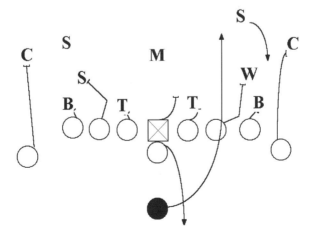

If the defense starts kicking over to one side on us we send the end in motion and bring him back to where he started from.

The first play you will see is our Toss Play. Everyone runs the Toss. Instead of just lining up in the I Formation we can spread the defense.

First we will look at our Running Game and then we will come back and go over our Passing Game and our Play-Action Passes.

I want to go over two passes that we use to complement ourselves off our Two-Tight-End look. These are all Play-Action passes. We run the play off the inside zone. Anytime we have the quarterback come outside on the naked situation and no one is pulling out to protect him we always have someone dragging across the back side. The onside tight end will Buzz block for three counts and then release to the flat. The outside receiver runs a flag route while the other receiver runs the post. He looks for the high receiver first and then he looks for the high low to the two tight ends. We always have an offside receiver run the back-side post to keep the Safety from coming up on the end crossing over underneath.

On the next play we will fake the Counter Trap and run the same routes. Now we have the guard and tackle pulling outside with the quarterback. It is a Play-Action Pass that complements our run.

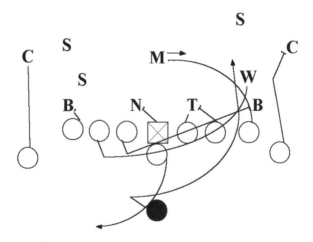

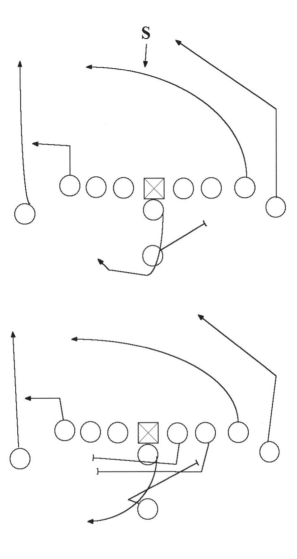

We get in this formation and sprint the quarterback out. We drag the back-side end at 10 to 12 yards. On the sprint-out situation the back has to cut the defensive end man on the line so the tight end does not have to Buzz block before he releases. Now he can release to the flat. The two outside receivers run a combination route. The inside man runs an out route at about 12 yards. The outside man runs a nine or deep route. The quarterback rolls out and looks for the nine man deep first. If the deep man is not open he looks for the high low underneath.

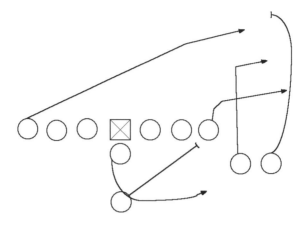

We also run a delay route. This is not a play-action pass. We set the tight end and have him block for three counts. He releases over the middle and gets behind the Mike linebacker. The wideout on the right side runs a back-side dig route. The other wideout runs a front-side post. The other tight end runs a crossing route. We are looking to throw the ball to the delay man.

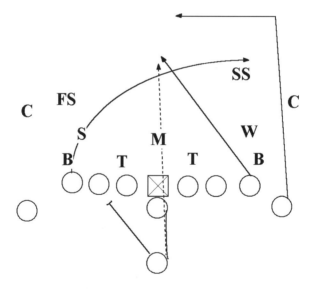

We also run some combo routes that are not play action. We have been running the toss sweep and counter trap and now we run a pass with a two-man game on that side. The man on the line will run a flag route. The wing will drive off 7 or 8 yards to the outside and then settle. Now he reads the defense. If he reads man coverage he comes sliding across toward the center. If he reads zone he is going to sit down right there and do a hook. Over on the other side we run a high-low combo.

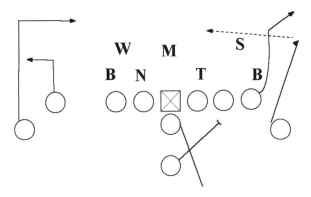

The other thing we do is to run the same play from our motion with the end. We see a lot of man free coverage and a lot of man under. We bring the man off the line and bring him in motion and he runs the delay route.

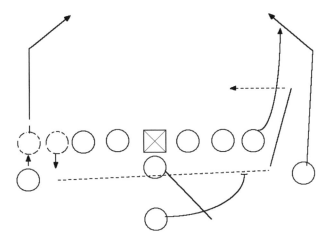

Chapter 2

LINE BLOCKING SCHEMES

By
Mike Cummings
Central Michigan University
1995

I will show you three main blocking schemes that we use to move the ball on the ground. We refer to them as a Base, Lead, and a Gap Scheme. We try to keep our blocking scheme as simple as possible.

BASE BLOCK

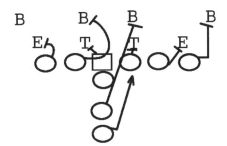

The second scheme we use is our Lead Blocking Scheme for inside running plays. In this scheme our offensive linemen will Zone block. They will all step toward the point of attack and block the man in that zone. The adjacent linemen all work toward the play side and are responsible to block the defender in their frontside gap or the adjacent lineman's backside gap.

LEAD BLOCK INSIDE

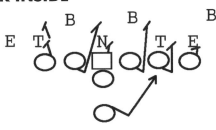

We also use a Lead Blocking Scheme for an outside play. The offensive linemen use zone blocking principles in this scheme as well. However, the zone they will work through is designated differently to account for the outside course of the ball carrier. The linemen still step toward the play side and block the zone and man in that zone, and still have the adjacent backside lineman covering their backside gap.

LEAD BLOCK OUTSIDE

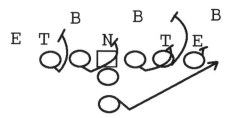

The third blocking scheme we use to run the football is our Gap Blocking Scheme. This is also a zone blocking scheme, but in this scheme our linemen will step away from the point of attack and work toward the back side of the play. We will leave a defender to be trapped/logged on the front side. We can trap with our fullback, guard, center, or tackle.

GAP BLOCK

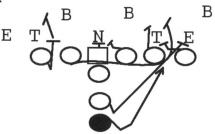

What is most relevant and important to all these schemes is not how each play is blocked precisely against each front. It is the techniques involved in each scheme that make it so successful. It is our ability to practice them, drill them, correct them the greatest number of times while still becoming more and more aggressive. The greatest concern is how to practice and drill these techniques that make the scheme work so well.

I will give you the techniques that we use at the point of attack in each of our three main schemes (Base, Lead, Gap), and I will show you what we use as our base drills to develop these schemes while we develop our linemen. I will give particular attention to the combination blocks and the points we emphasize on each of these.

There are some concerns with using three different blocking schemes. The biggest concern, besides simply to teach them, is the raising of the pad level on the Lead Schemes. Leverage is not only a commodity at your place, but at ours as well. We are concerned with our players playing higher on Lead Schemes than they do on Base and Gap Schemes.

ZONE/LEAD

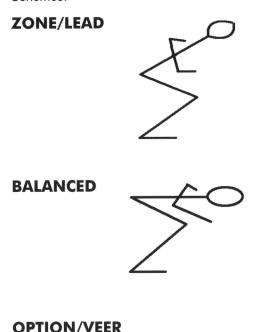

BALANCED

OPTION/VEER

We understand that the Lead Schemes cause offensive linemen to play with their pads somewhat higher than in Gap or Base Schemes, but we don't want them *much* higher. We especially don't want our linemen to *think* that they should be playing higher. We develop our linemen to knock people off the ball *first*, then we get into other stuff. We *will not* bump and shove. We use boards and chutes; every day we work on leverage. We teach, we indoctrinate, we demand leverage first; if your linemen learn to play low and play hard first, you can teach them Zone blocking. But if you teach Zone blocking first, you're going to have a problem getting them into a good mind-set on short yardage and goal line to knock someone off the ball.

If we only used Lead Schemes (Zone Run), we would have a different philosophy on our teaching of run blocking and leverage. Our offensive philosophy dictates that we do this (run everything) so we feel we must work on the toughest aspect of blocking first, which is leverage. Then we work on Lead Schemes and Gap Schemes and employ the principles of leverage to these schemes.

Let me talk about blocking in general. We talk about going back to the basics when talking about blocking. Blocking can be improved to a greater degree than any other phase of the game. Let me list these basics concerning blocking.

1. STANCE—Fit what you do offensively: power = narrow; balance = wide. We must be able to do it all from the stance.

2. FEET/FOOTWORK—Emphasize frequency, not length (don't pick them up too high, losing frequency). Kill the cat? Pound the feet on the ground. Teach where the first, second, and third steps should go: *WHY*? The offensive lineman can't take a wrong step. Give them landmarks and aiming points. Make contact on the second step (never on the first step). The first step is timing and weight transfer; the second step is power, and then punch.

3. SURFACE—Identify the surface to be used; helmet, hands, shoulder/forearm. Aim point w/surface. Give the offensive lineman part of the defender's body to aim at for the best chance (shoulder, hip, sternum—be specific). Our general rule is this: hands at the point of attack, control. Shoulder forearm — BS = Power.

4. FIT POSITION—It is a constant struggle to keep the knees bent and the butt up. Gather ability; adjust ability. It is important to keep the back flat on contact. The hips will roll naturally. We teach the stalemate: rolling the hips *isn't* the key.

5. REPETITION—We do the same drills every day. We make the drills fit our scheme and technique. Conditioning is achieved by going full speed. We want more reps than any other player. The tough part is practice; the game is easy. Again, consistency is our goal.

6. MOTIVATION—Individual and team goals are used. We want measurable goals. Our goal is to be the "Best line in the Mid-American Conference." When we grade our film we give extra credit on blocking. We can give it and we can take it away. A Pancake or Knockdown block gets extra credit.

7. ENTHUSIASM—The coach has to build enthusiasm. We can grind them, run them, and then we must love them. We want to know

them as individuals because they will play harder if they feel close to the group. The more we know about them the more we can help them. If we know them as individuals we can tell if they are having a good day or not. We must make the right things important. If everything is important, then nothing is important. There are certain things to pick out that are important.

8. PATIENCE—We feel this is very important. How would you want your child to be treated? Every once in a while kids need a kick in the rear. We run a tight ship. We set the rules early and stay with them.

9. BLOCKING TRIANGLE—This is our philosophy on blocking. We want them to know WHO to block. We want to make it simple for them. We stress these three points: WHO—HOW—AGGRESSIVE!

BLOCKING TRIANGLE

10. KEEP IT SIMPLE—We have a 20-hour rule in college and we can not spend a lot of time doing nothing. The 20 hours include the games and everything else we do. We want to knock people off the ball. It is easier said than done. We want to run north and south to win. If things are not working we subtract a play instead of adding more plays. Also, we do less talking and spend more time on the practice field.

I will show you how we teach each point of attack technique and how we drill it.

Our Base Block is a Man Block and is used primarily at the point of attack. We tell our linemen who have the assignment of base blocking that the ball carrier is directly behind him and will make his cut depending on which way he takes the defender. In our Base Block we allow our offensive lineman to take the defender any way he wants to go. That is the block used on our basic Isolation play.

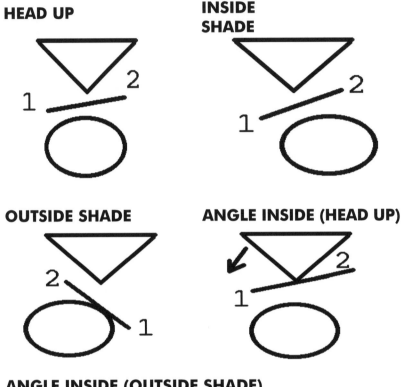

HEAD UP

INSIDE SHADE

OUTSIDE SHADE

ANGLE INSIDE (HEAD UP)

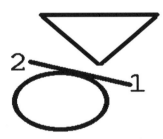

ANGLE INSIDE (OUTSIDE SHADE)

The first step is with the inside foot, or near foot. The inside foot is used if the defender is head up or inside. We will step with the near foot if the defender is outside. The first step should get the offensive lineman square to the defender and not to the line of scrimmage. The first step should be halfway to the defender, and make contact on the second step.

The second step is upfield at the defender. We make contact on the second step. We are already square to the defender, so we want to get into the defender. Our first step will take care of any slant or angle. We punch on our second step at the defender.

The aiming point for our headgear is the sternum of the defender. We will focus into the sternum to see any movement. It is the middle of the defender, and we can continue contact regardless of movement of the defender.

The surface we aim for is the helmet and hands. We want to punch and shock the defender and get control. We want to maintain a flat back, tail slightly higher than our shoulders. We get on the insteps with high frequency. Drive the defender by driving the knees inside. Our hips will roll with movement of the defender. We Base Block primarily on Isolation plays.

ISOLATION PLAY

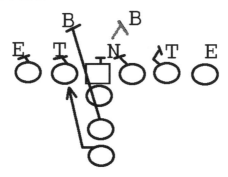

Next is our Lead Blocking or Zone Blocking. We use a "Pick" blocking scheme when our ball carrier is using an inside course; and the cut may go inside or outside the combination block on the front side. Let me go over the Lead Blocker. His first step is in the bucket; then he turns his shoulders far enough so that the second step comes down on the ground at the crotch of the defender. The second step is on the ground at the crotch of the defender; the punch comes through on the second step. The second step designates the zone. We refer to this as the Track. We want to stay on Track.

We use the hands and helmet if the defender slants to the lead blocker. We use the shoulder and forearm if the defender angles away. We want to finish the block. We stay on course unless we are using a scoop block by the trail blocker. The ball carrier makes his cut off of the combination block. If the scoop is used, we stay on course to the linebacker. Once he is on the linebacker he has him man to man.

Let me go over the Trail Blocker. His first step is in the bucket. He turns his shoulders enough so that on the second step he can contact the ground while being pointed at the crotch of the defender. We want to establish "Tandem" relationship, or get the trail blocker behind the lead blocker. The second step in underneath his own hip. It will be pointed at the defender's crotch, with the play-side hand extended.

Next we look at what happens when the READS take place. 1) *SCOOP* if defender is coming inside; shove the lead blocker off and helmet adjust to defender's play-side number and take the defender over. 2) *BASE* if the defender is going outside, continue on zone (tracks), established by the second step on the way to the linebacker. On the slant course by the tailback we use the shoulder and forearm. On the cutback by the tailback we use the helmet and hands. 3) *SHOVE/ DOUBLE* if the defender is hanging inside but has not declared inside or outside, shove with the hand over to the lead blocker. Double-team while staying on course to the linebacker.

PICK INSIDE PLAY

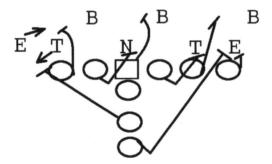

Next are our Lead Schemes. We use the Scoop Block on outside running plays. The ball carrier is going outside the combination block. We have two blockers: Lead and Trail. On the first step the lead blocker drop-steps and turns his shoulders enough to get the second step on the ground just inside the play-side foot to the defender. We may lose more ground if the defender is farther outside. We lose ground to gain ground.

On the second step we contact the ground at a point just inside the play-side foot of the defender. Contact is made on the second step, and we want to establish a zone, or tracks. We want to knock the defender off the ball.

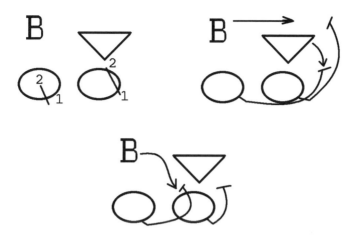

We use our hands to the helmet to the play-side number of the defenders on defensive linemen or the linebacker. We use a shoulder forearm against fast-flowing linebackers. To finish the block we bring the play-side arm into the outside of the defender's play-side number and maintain a lateral position. When scooped off, we maintain lateral position on the linebacker with the strong play-side arm.

Our trail blocker's first step is a drop step. He turns his shoulder enough so that on the second step he contacts the ground underneath his own hip with his foot pointed at the inside of the defender's play-side foot. The second step is underneath his hip point at the inside of the defender's play-side foot, with the play-side hand extended. On the second step the trail blocker will read the man on the lead blocker. He "feels" the linebacker.

To finish he brings his hand into the ribs and shoves the adjacent offensive lineman off to go to the front-side linebacker. He adjusts his helmet to the defender's play-side number, and takes over the defensive lineman with the strong play-side hand and helmet adjust.

Our third blocking scheme is our Gap Scheme. We double-team at the point of attack.

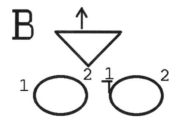

We trap with the fullback or guard (center). We use a *"swipe"* combination/double team on our Gap Scheme when we have a trap by a fullback or guard, and an off-tackle aiming point by our ball carrier. We use a Zone Scheme away from the point of attack.

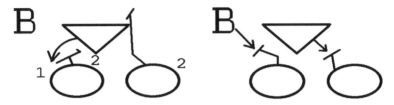

We use two blockers: the Lead or Chipper, and the Trail or Swiper. The Lead Blocker is referred to as the chipper. On his first step he slides and steps inside. The slide should be far enough to get the second step down on the ground in the crotch of the defensive lineman. If the defender is aligned such that the second step would go in the crotch now, he will use a settle or weight transfer step and gain no ground inside. On the second step we contact the ground at the defender's crotch. As contact is made on the second step we establish the zone on the second step and work straight upfield.

We want the shoulder and forearm on the surface of the defender. We want the head out of the block, with the eyes on the backside linebacker.

On the Finish we want to take a waddle step and knock the defensive lineman straight back off the ball. We want to stay into the defensive linemen until we are on the linebacker level. We keep the surface on the defensive lineman as long as possible.

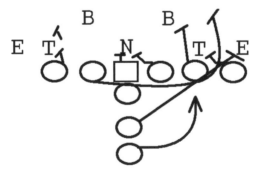

The Trail Blocker is the Swiper. His first step is a lateral and upfield/lead step at the inside of the defensive lineman's play-side foot. We gain ground to get to the defender. The lead blocker is ahead of him.

He must keep his shoulders square to the linebacker. His second step is upfield. He should bring his feet to a parallel position (toe to toe). The second step cannot be past the parallel position or it will cause a Down Block on the defensive lineman and squeeze the chipper off his block.

On the blocking surface we want the helmet on the play-side number with the hands inside on the man's shoulder pads with the stronger play-side arm. To finish the block we want to knock the defensive lineman off the ball, straight back. We tell him to block the defensive lineman as if he had no help. If the defensive lineman angles inside, he must stay on course and work upfield to the linebacker.

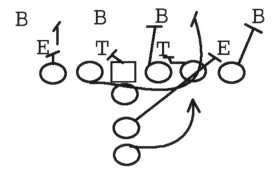

Chapter 3

BASIC PASS PROTECTION SCHEMES

By
Tom Freeman
University of Pittsburgh
1998

I want to talk a little about our basic pass protection. In the NFL the hardest thing for defensive coaches to do is to break down the pass protections. If they figure out where your protections are, and if you are sitting there with only one protection, come the fourth quarter they are going to get you. We know their stunts and dogs will beat every protection.

You must have the ability to throw the ball from a variety of formations and from a variety of personnel groupings. Also, you must be able to do these things with different pass protections. It gets into a guessing game contest.

Several years ago I had the opportunity to hear Buddy Ryan talk about the time the Bears won the Super Bowl. All Coach Ryan wanted to know about your offense was how you pass protected on your first possession of the game. He did that because he knew that was your first choice of pass protection schemes. At that time offensive teams would go from Man, to Slides, to Zones, to try to stay one step ahead of Buddy. That was hard to do because he was sharp. He knew how you started the game and he knew you would go back to it in the fourth quarter. He had the stunts and blitzes that would get you.

The tough thing about college football today is that you must have more than a couple of pass protection schemes. The defensive coaches are getting smarter by the day.

In our basic pass protection we want to put our two backs on the least likely pass rushers. We have the fullback responsible for the Sam linebacker, the tailback is responsible for the Will linebacker, and the down linemen have the four down linemen and the Mike linebacker. The Sam linebacker may well be a stand-up rush-type end. We declare to the four down defensive men and the Mike linebacker. This is our Split Flow Seven-Man Pass Protection.

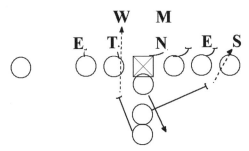

A protection that we have come back to is a Seven-Man Single Back Protection. This is used when we run a weak flood or a weak flow pass. Now, all we are doing is putting the fullback as the lead blocker. The tight end takes the fullback's responsibility. The line blocking remains the same. They have the four down linemen and the Mike linebacker.

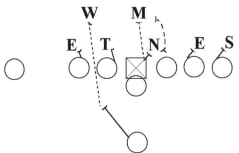

If we come up against an even defense we do not want to send the tackle out on the linebacker. The tackle sits inside and looks for the linebacker. The tight end sits on the defensive end. If the Sam linebacker drops we pop our tackle out and pick the defensive end up. We make a "GO" call to get the tackle out on the end.

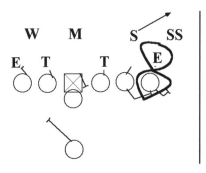

If they run the stunt with the Sam linebacker coming inside, the tackle picks up the tackle and the guard takes the linebacker. This gets tough to do. The reason is the tight ends are half tackles and half wide receivers. Now I have made them half pass blockers. Fortunately we get help from the tackle for the end.

We do have a call to help the end. If the wide man on the line is cheating outside he can tell the tackle to block inside and he will block outside. We can run this from a One-Back or a Two-Back Set. If we run from a Two-Back Set the tailback releases on his route and the fullback picks up the Will linebacker.

Let me show you our basic Six-Man Protection. I will go through all the things we see against the Fire Zones. Our Six-Man Protection is a Slide Protection where the fullback, or the remaining back, is responsible for two men. The fullback reads the number 1 man first and the second man next. If both backers come, the quarterback has to throw the ball quick to the Hot receiver.

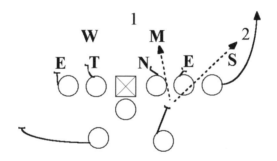

On the left side the left tackle has the C Gap Weak, the left guard has the B Gap Weak, and the center has A Gap Weak. On the right side the right guard has A Gap Strong, the tackle has the C Gap Strong, and the fullback has 1 first and 2 second. It is Zone Pass Protection. I will talk about these sets because they are a little different than what you have on your solid seven-man protection. This protection is very much akin to your basic Sprint Draw blocking.

Next is the Slide Protection against an even front. We see a lot of this defense. We are going to slide to the weak side. The center has the A Gap. The guard has the B Gap defender, and the tackle has the C Gap defender. We have the other guard take the tackle, and our tackle takes the end. The remaining back has the double read on the linebackers.

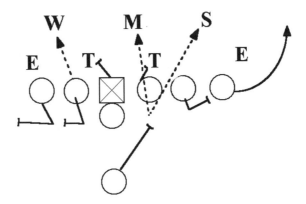

I know there are a lot of stunts the defense can run against this defense. This is a real flexible protection scheme. That is a quick overview of our basic pass protection.

When we run our Three-Step Drop Game we can run it with any protection by simply putting the THREE in front of it. For example, our Split-Flow Protection is 84 and 85. If we want to run our Split-Flow Seven-Man Check Release Pass Protection all we say is 384 or 385. Our Weak Flood Protection is 78 and 79. Most of the time we run the Speed play as 378 or 379. We also block our 60 and 61 rules with Three-Step tempo. We must do a better job with our tackles of getting to the defense to make them get their hands out. We had a pass knocked down in the bowl game. They should run-block the inside half of the defender they are responsible for.

If we were in a formation where we are spread out, there is another Three-Step Drop Protection we would use. It would be special protection. I would glad to talk with you later on this.

We are going to be more than just a one protection team. We have a way to take the Six-Man Protection to a Five-Man Protection. We have a way to take the Solid Seven-Man Protection to a Six-Man Protection. We only use about four or five varieties. Now, you do not go into a game with all of these protections. Against a lot of these defenses the protection ends up being identical. It comes down to a matter of time restraints and what your kids can handle. I know we have more time with our kids than you do. High school kids play both ways a lot, but our kids only play one way. But we still must be careful what we do with them.

Here is a standard Fire Zone Defense that we see. Most Fire Zones come from the field side. The first defense we look at is the Under defense, or the Eagle defense.

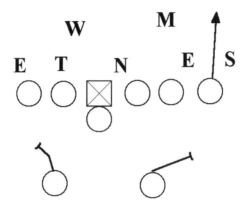

This is the same defense drawn to a Twins Formation. It is to the wide side of the field.

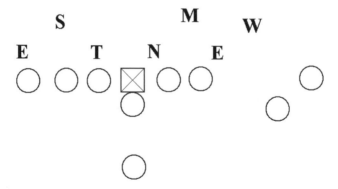

If we are in our base pass protection which is 85 or 84, with Split Flow, the end is going out on a pattern. The fullback takes the end man. If we are in Split Backs our backs are up and they have a chance to see the linebacker and they should know when it is coming. The tailback checks off the Will. By rule the linemen have the End, Tackle, Nose, the End, and the Mike.

Now, let me talk about some techniques in this protection. If you get burned on something you learn from it. We got burned on this stunt when I was coaching at Purdue and we played up at Wisconsin. We used to bring the near-side guard down to help on the nose all of the time. The Mike linebacker came inside and our guard could not get back outside to pick him up and he got in our backfield. In practice we could block the crap out of the scout team. But when we got in the game we could not pick him up. We learned from that point on that instead of Zone Blocking that stunt, we are going to Man Block that stunt.

Now, instead of the guard stepping down to help the center with the nose we set him back off the ball. He looks at the Mike linebacker. If the linebacker drops and they are playing a straight defense the guard will come back inside to help with the nose. We want to know where the hip of the over nose is. By doing this we knock the defense out of the pass rush lane. Again, you learn from your mistakes. We went back to blocking that stunt with Man protection.

The thing we harp to our kids about is this: Most defensive teams are going to be disciplined in their pass rush lanes. We get back off the ball and give ourselves a chance to help inside or outside.

Most teams will give their stunts away. They will cheat a man on one side or the other, or move him inside or outside. I tell our guys that it is my job to send them into the game with the best chance to block any stunt. If I can pick up that tip and pass it on that is what I should do. If I am on offense and the fullback only goes to his left when he puts his left hand down, then we need to know that. We look for tips from the defense the same way. The thing we must remember is that the defense has smart guys coaching them, too. I would love to Zone Block the stunt every time.

We have put the center on an island. We tell him to trust his buddies. We are going to give him help when we can. If the nose loops to the backside on the center he must redirect on the play.

On the backside, even though the end is lined up wide, eventually he will cross the face of our tackle. This is what we tell our tackle. The first thing the tackle must be aware of is the Corner Blitz. A lot of teams will bring the Corner and Will and drop the end. The end sneaks a peek to see if the Corner is coming. If the Corner is not coming we tell our guy to drop-step and go help the guard. The reason it is imperative that he drop-steps is because we want our guard to knock the defender into the tackle. Once the tackle is locked on the defender, the guard can come back and help the center. There is a good chance help will come. The problem is that some teams will run the stunt and bring both the end and linebacker. They have all kinds of combinations. We do not always pick them up the way we would like. We tell the center any help he gets is a bonus.

From the start we teach our tackles if they have a 5 technique on them and the guard is uncovered, any help the tackle gets will be late. The guard's first move is to set back and help the center. If our line can understand the scheme and what is going on they should get into position where they can help.

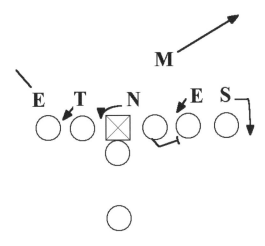

Here is a hint for the backs blocking on linebackers. If the back will take the first step with his inside foot he will be in position to block the linebacker When they get fancy and want to step with that out-side foot first they will miss the block if the linebacker comes inside. He must know the linebacker he is responsible for and then he wants to step right at him with his inside foot. As he reads the release he can still get out of the backfield.

If I am the right tackle I have to look at the defender's eyes every time. If I am looking at his eyes it means I have my eyes up. I can see what is happening. If the man is looking inside and then goes inside, now the tackle has a chance to help the quarterback.

Most of the Fire Zones that we see come out of the Three-Man Front Schemes. It may be a 3-4 look, or the Under look. If we are in a Twin Set it becomes an Over look.

If we are in our base Split Flow Pass Protection the tight end is outside. By rule the tackle has the end, the guard has the tackle, the center and guard have the nose and Mike linebacker, the tackle has the tackle, and the tailback has the Will linebacker. The strong back has the Sam linebacker.

It is the same principle. The tackle is sitting on the end. If he drops off, the tackle looks to see if the strong safety is coming. If not, he drop-steps and gets back inside to help the guard.

We tell the guard if his man loops hard, if he gets him knocked back on the tackle, he can help inside. We tell them not to screw yourself to help your buddy. We want to make sure the tackle has the man before the guard leaves to help inside. We stress for them to get on a man and stay on him.

When the defense is crossing the stunts with the line and linebackers I can't emphasize it enough. You can Zone block with a back and a lineman. Whoever gets there first must get his hands on the man and stick with him. He must be decisive. The lineman must let the backs know who they are blocking and let him adjust to the lineman. If you do that you will have a chance on this.

Now I want to talk about picking up the twist stunt. Let me go through our base philosophy on handling the twist. When we come to the line of scrimmage and see two adjacent down linemen we want to tell them what is going on. We think of the possibility of the twist. This has a lot to do with down and distance. We refer to the first man as the Power Rusher. All that man is doing is giving up his body to free the second man. The loop man is the guy they are trying to get home. If they run the tackle and end on a twist, we call it a tight-end stunt. If the end is going first and the tackle second we call it ET. Some teams call those stunts Tango, and all kinds of other names. We call them what they are—ET and TE.

We want to flatten the power rusher or the man who goes first. We want to get our hands on that man and knock him down the line. We want to flatten him out down the line. The blocker who knows it is a twist is the man that has the loop man. The twist man will stand up and show you his numbers before he makes his move around the rusher. Now, it is the job of the second blocker to force the switch. He must snap his eyes and head to make the block. The fastest way to turn the head is to snap your eyes. He snaps his eyes and drop-steps and comes down the line and forces the switch. We let the line call out "switch, switch, switch." But we do not want to hear them say they did not hear the switch call when they come to the sideline.

We tell the man on the power rush that we want him to deliver the man on the switch. We do not want him to pass him down, we want him to deliver him to the blocker. Coach Larry Marmie used to love that term. Once the inside man gets the bump, the tackle must drop-step and come back off the ball.

This is how we have always taught this. We take a drill and teach them the basic set to start out with. Then when we run our stunts we do not trick them to begin with. We flat tell them what the defense is going to do. We walk them through the blocks, then we jog them, and then we will go full speed. We take two guys and work with them on each stunt. Then we will go full speed without telling them what is going on. Give them a chance to have some success. It is like coach Glen Mason said: Success breeds success. We want to give them some confidence as they learn to block the twist. We tell them to see the twist but not to look at it.

Chapter 4

OFFENSIVE LINE PLAY

By
Dan Haley
Bowling Green (Ky.) High School
1996

My topic is Offensive Line Play. I will start out by providing a context from which our ideas have evolved. First, I want to tell you this is not a scheme talk. If you want to get out of here you can. This is not a scheme lecture. It is not a philosophy talk about all of the things we believe in. Best of all, this is not a talk where a coach comes up and puts on a ton of overlays with a list of 10 things we are going to do. This is going to be a "Technique Talk." I will cover in detail the feet, eyes, and head, and how-to-deliver-a-blow talk. I am not trying to tell you this is the best way to teach or coach offensive linemen or how to teach the drive block. I am saying what I think is the best way to teach the drive block.

We have been a Triple-Option Football Team for more than 20 years now. We went through the Split-Back Veer Era and the Wishbone Era. As the defenses adjusted and caught up, we tried to evolve the offense rather than ditch the concept altogether. The main reason we have embraced the offense and stayed with it over the years is the Blocking Scheme. It allows us to block with five people on four people. It allows us to come off the football at full throttle. What I am saying is that the way we teach blocking is a function of the offense that we run. With a different scheme we might believe different things, but for our scheme we believe in the following six points:

1) We use a three-point stance with our weight equally distributed.

2) At the line of scrimmage our down hand is grounded three inches from the neutral zone; not back like most teams. We are up on the line crowding the line of scrimmage.

3) We use the snap count to get a jump on the defense.

4) We want to explode in the face of the defense. We want to explode a vertical release through the aiming point, somewhere on someone's body. We want to make a vertical release to an aiming point to what we call a level 5. That is just 5 yards downfield. Level 1, 2, 3, 4, and 5 are the number of yards downfield we strive for.

5) We make a commitment with our players that we are going to come off the football better than anyone else in football. We are going to measure this commitment. We look at the films and show them coming off the line of scrimmage. The way we measure this is by checking the feet on the snap of the football. We want 11 feet moving on the snap of the football. We want to see 11 sets of feet moving on the ground before you can see any evidence of the defense reacting. That is what we mean by coming off the football.

6) We believe we have to knock a hole in the defense. From that hole we are going to attack horizontally and vertically. Those are the principles we operate on.

We teach several types of blocks, and several blocking combinations, but everything we do in the running game is based upon the Drive Block. I want to take you through the coaching points and some drills that we use in teaching the Drive Block. Then I want to take those principles and use them to develop the Zone Blocking Combination as we teach it.

In the Drive Block we start with Stance and Start. We simply believe that a three-point stance allows us to be more explosive than a four-point stance. We think a four-point stance rounds the shoulders more, and rounded shoulders tend to round the back, and a rounded back diminishes explosiveness.

We believe in the three-point stance. We teach it with the toes at 12 inches and the heels at 13 inches, which makes us slightly pigeon-toed. We have a slight foot stagger. Why do we want to be narrow in our stance? We want to be narrow in our stance because it facilitates a better takeoff, and being slightly pigeon-toed allows for better push-off, especially when taking a slight angle. We want to move forward. If you watch most sprinters in track you can see how they get down. They have a narrow base because they want to go forward. We want the ankles close and the Z's in the knees. We want the hips "Cocked" into what we call a Power Position, slightly higher than the shoulders, and hand placement such that the natural line or sight for the eyes is a point on the ground 1 ½ yards in front of that hand. We call that point on the ground the "Basic Spot" for the eyes.

We do go at angles. We have to take that fact into account. The reason we are slightly pigeon-toed is so when we are not going forward we can make that step at an angle. If we are going to the right we want to step with the near foot, just as most of you do. We want to attack with the near foot. If we are going to the left we want to lead with the left foot first.

When you strike a blow, regardless if you are a tackler or blocker, there are two components. There is the Power that goes into it, and the Explosion that comes on top of it. I use Hank Aaron as an example to our players. He weighed 165 pounds, but when he swung the baseball bat he was generating Power. When he got the wrist turned he got the Explosion into the swing. That was how he was able to hit more than 700 home runs. So, when we are blocking we want Power and Explosion. I want them coordinated. We tell our kids the Power comes from the waist down. The Power comes from the butt and the legs. The Explosion comes from the upper body.

The question is this: If all of the power comes from the lower body, how do you get the Power into the Explosion? The answer is this: It has to be transferred just like electricity right through the body. The Power of the lower body, if it is going to get into the blow, must come through the trunk of the body. If the trunk of the body is rounded it will not go through. It is just like lifting weights. On the Dead Lift we can get 500 pounds on the Olympic Bar. They can't just reach over and pick up the 500 pounds. You have 500 pounds in the lower body and it has to come through the trunk. If you get the back in a power position and get your hips under the bar you can come straight up and get those 500 pounds.

It is fundamental in the winter program. Make sure they learn how to get down in position. We do not want the banana back. That position is a non-aggressive position. He can't hit from that position. We want the head to be an extension of the body. We want the eyes to be focused on what we call the Basic Spot. The basic spot for the eyes is 1½ yards in front of the hand. We tell them to look through their eyebrows to the Basic Spot. We keep our free arm on the knee. We do not carry it sidesaddle. We feel it makes us more explosive; it may not be, but that is our thinking.

We tell our players to "store" the snap count in their memory, and then concentrate on the ultimate objective of their assignment. We want them to concentrate on their assignment. We want them to concentrate on their objective and allow the snap count to "trigger" them. The

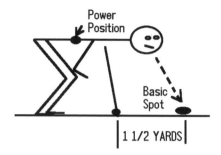

definition of Concentration is ONENESS—One Thought. We do not want them to concentrate on the snap count. We want them to concentrate on the objective they have on the play. We want them to concentrate on what they are asked to do on the play.

We try to get on the defense before they can move. Everyone has a prescribed first step, and we take pride in getting it on the ground before there is any noticeable defensive reaction. We want to come off the ball better than anyone in football and attack aiming points.

Let's talk about the Drive Block. I will break the block down into three components: the Approach, Contact, and Follow-Through.

First is the Approach. We come out of the stance with a four-inch step. We come off hard but we don't want to overstride. I have talked about the concentration that gets you out of your stance. When we come out of our basic stance our eyes go from the Basic Spot to the Landmark. The Landmark is the aiming point of the defender we are attacking. That will be the breastbone or the play-side number, depending on the play called. When we Drive Block we will not aim at the armpit or the knee; we are aiming at the breastbone or the play-side number. We want their eyes to go from the Basic Spot to the Landmark in 0 seconds. It is HIKE—Bam! There is no in between. I will stress one additional point. Coach Blanton Collier always said, "The most important thing in blocking is the eyes." He was a brilliant coach and a great technician. When I started coaching I used this point. "The most important thing in blocking is the eyes." I was not sure about this when I first started coaching. Over the years I have become a firm believer in this point.

We come out of our stance with a four-inch step. We come off hard, but we don't want to overstride. If we overstride on the first step it is difficult for us to adjust to an aiming point that moves laterally. With a four-inch first step we can adjust to lateral defensive movement and still strike the target vertically. The short first step makes it physically possible to block movement, but the key to doing it lies with the eyes. The most important thing in blocking is the EYES. Eyes tell your feet what to do, and eyes time the delivery of the block. We want the eyes to go from the Basic Spot to the Aiming Point in the instant of the first movement. The EYES are the blocker's guidance system.

The first step gets us in the frame of the defender, and the second step establishes the Base Spot. Film studies clearly show that offensive linemen who don't establish base with the second step lose balance on the third step. Some players have more trouble than others, but I believe a significant part of coaching the Drive Block is the coaching of the second step. In addition to blocking on the boards every day, we have a little "Block Movement" drill that we do at "Thud" speed that helps us train the feet, so they respond to what their eyes tell them.

A blocker may Step-hit, Step-step-hit, or Step-step-step-hit, but regardless of the distance he must travel, he is in the "Delivery Area" when he is within three steps of the defender. In the hit area, he must eye the target, be on track, in frame, beneath the target plane, hips lower than the head, and in a power position, and all levers cocked. We say he comes into a hitting position. His head should be an extension of his body.

We call the area we are aiming for the Target Plane. We want the blocker to approach the target in the Delivery Area where he can block the defender. He must be lower than the Target Plane. He must keep his eyes on the target.

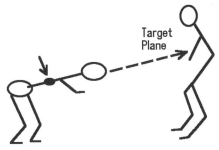

Target Plane

When he comes out of his stance and attacks the defender, he must be beneath the man, his eyes must be on the target, and his hips must be lower than his head. His feet must be on track. His body must be on his frame, and he must be in a power position in his hips.

Next is Contact. As the eyes tell the feet what to do, they also tell the body when to deliver the blow. As the blocker enters the "Delivery Area," the eyes say when the hips should roll under, steps shorten, body extend, and power transfer to the hitting surface. Then the eyes say when the upper body should explode into the target. If the blocker eyes the target, and if all the levers are in the right place, then the blocker generates tremendous power and explodes it up through the aiming point with perfect timing.

The aiming point for a Drive Block should be either the breastbone or the play-side number. The blocker should deliver an ascending blow, up through it, and movement will occur. The blow is delivered with the pads and hands.

If the blocker delivers the blow properly, the defender will be moved backward. Now comes the Follow-Through. To finish the block and drive him vertically backward, the blocker must sustain the pressure of the initial blow with strong leg drive. We coach him to "Hit through and sustain," working upward as he goes.

It takes more power to cause movement than to sustain it, so the blocker must trade some power for balance as he drives the defender backward. He should widen his base slightly and work up as he drives. He cannot give his man the opportunity to recover or disengage. We like to finish the block with our man in the reach position. Being physically superior is a tremendous advantage, but hard work on quality repetitions will develop mechanics that, coupled with toughness and effort, can make an average player into an excellent blocker.

Let's look at Blocking Combinations that we get into. I will go over the Veer against the 4-3 defense. The rule for our offensive linemen on the back side of the Veer play is "Zone Play-side Gap" or Z.P.G. That means that each player is responsible for blocking the defender who is responsible for the play-side gap. Usually, there is a lineman and a linebacker in the area, aligned so that they could switch their gap control from one play to the next. We want to "Zone Them," or come off the ball and pick them up regardless of how they react.

On the front side we have two basic rules. First, we want to collapse the "3 Technique" area. Second, we do not want any leakage on the front side when we run the Veer. On the back side everyone is Zone Blocking to the onside gap. Those are the two basic blockers I want to cover.

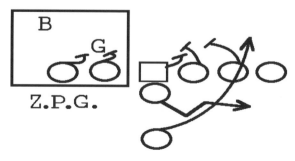

Let's take a 4-3 defense for example, and let's Z.P.G with our left guard and left tackle as we would do if the play went to the right. We would operate on the assumption that the "Two Technique" and the Will linebacker would become backside "A" and "B" for defenders on the flow away. If "Will" scraped to the backside "A Gap" then the "Two Technique" would defend the backside "B Gap" for the cut-back. We want our backside guard to block the "A Gap" defender, and our backside tackle to block the "B Gap" defender.

The guard attacks the play-side arm pit of the "Two Technique," using Drive Blocking principles. The tackle attacks the breastbone of the "Two," also with a Drive Block principle. With the eyes leading the way, the guard picks up the "A Gap" defender in the "V" of his left shoulder. They drive to level 5 without permitting the defenders to cross their blocks.

If you are primarily a running football team I do not think you can run the Veer from a Split-Back Alignment. With the defenses today you will have a hard time outnumbering the alignments on the corner. We have embraced the Three-Back Triple Option Concept. We do not want to line up in the Three-Back Set because it places restrictions on the Passing Game. We line up in the Broken Bone alignment a lot. Our two basic schemes against a 50 Defense as far as blocking is concerned are these. If the tackle is in a 5 Technique on the call side, and we make a "5 Call" we are going to Drive Block on the linebacker and nose. It is a "three-on-two" situation. We explode the fullback off the hip of the guard and read the tackle first and the end second.

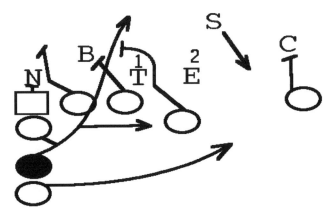

If the defense has two men outside in the secondary, we have a problem. If we bring the ball outside we have only one blocker block-ing on two defenders. One of the defenders will come up and one will be deep. The wideout must block the defender who comes up. You have to live with the other man if you are going to run the play into that defense.

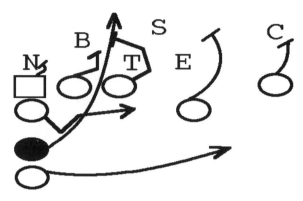

If the defensive tackle is in a "4 Technique" and we make a "4 Call," the tackle will step around the "4 Technique" and the Slot will arc outside on the deep man inside. We are in a better situation now because we can block two on two on the outside. We still Z.P.G. on the back side. Those are the two basic schemes we use against the 50 Defense. You know there is a lot more to the offense than this. You must have an adjustment for each situation. The basic block is the Drive Block, and the Zone Block fits in with the scheme. This is where it all starts from. We want to knock a hole in the defense, collapse the "3 Technique," and prevent leakage.

Chapter 5

LINE BLOCKING TECHNIQUES

By

Jerry Hanlon
University of Michigan
1991

How many times have you heard the comment that "Defense Wins Games"? If that statement was true then Bo Schembechler would have been coaching on that side of the football. He coached offense. *Offensive football is what wins games.* I want my offensive linemen to know that. If anyone wants to meet a real football player, then 90 percent of the time it is an offensive lineman. Think about this. The defensive coaches will grab a player and tell him to go in the game and stuff the offense for three plays, and then he can come back over on the bench and sit down. Hell, those kids don't get to play any football. I tell my players to stay out there for eight or 10 plays. I tell them to stay out there eight to 10 minutes if they want to play. I do not care how long they are on the field. I tell them just be sure to put some points on the board while they are out there. The only people who will know the offensive linemen are out on the field will be the moms, dads, uncles, and other relatives. It will not be their girlfriends because they are too damn ugly to have a girlfriend. That is the attitude the offensive line has to have. What are these guys looking for? They are looking for respect from their teammates. That is what we strive for and what we are looking for.

If you can teach blocking and teach technique you can move the football. What I want to move on to is how we teach some of the blocking techniques at Michigan. The first block is the Base Block. This is a One-on-One Block. You have to start to teach technique of any block with the stance. I have changed my viewpoint on the stance somewhat. I used to say I wanted my feet as far apart as the width of my armpits. Now I want the feet as wide as the shoulders. I have widened the stance somewhat. We did that because we pass the ball more. It is easier to get into the pass block fundamental position from a wider stance. To the side they put their hand down. I let them stagger their feet somewhat, not an awful lot, but I let them drop one foot back. I want about a heel-to-toe relationship.

Getting the offensive linemen into the proper position is extremely important. Everything starts with a good stance. I do not want them too comfortable in the stance, because I want them to get the hell out of it when the ball is snapped. I do not want comfort. I want effectiveness.

The next thing we teach is the buddy system. We have two players working together. The blocker has to know what it feels like to be in the perfect drive block position before he can make a perfect drive block. The partners work together to get into a form blocking position which teaches all the fundamentals of contact, leverage, and technique. When the blocker makes contact with his partner, he whips his fist up inside the shoulders of the defender. He leads with his forearms but brings his fist up inside. We have to center the head on the defender. We don't teach the butt block. We don't teach the shoulder block. If the defense would stand still we should teach a shoulder block. But they don't. Lead with the forearms, rip the fist up inside and center the helmet on the chest. The last thing is the follow-through. That comes when the defender tries to get off the block. The offense and defense may get into a stalemate. That is fine, because the defense must try to tackle the ball carrier. He is going to have to get rid of the blocker to make the tackle. When he attempts to do that, the follow-through takes place. The time to really get after the defense is when he tries to disengage with the blocker. That is when the blocker finishes his block.

The next block we teach is the Read technique. We use that technique when the defensive man is trying to seal him inside. I start from the basic stance. I am going to fire in such a way as to put my helmet right through the defender's outside hip. If the defender plays straight we have him in a shoulder block. If the defender plays the head of the offensive blocker, we are back in the base block. If the defender goes inside, we listen to the ancient Chinese philosopher, Confucius. Confucius say, "When one goes in, one goes out." The offensive blocker lets him go in and he goes out. He looks for the man outside. That is the linebacker scraping. That is the lead technique when the lineman is covered.

If the lineman is not covered and he is looking at the linebacker, he runs a different aiming point. His aiming point becomes the inside hip of the down lineman outside him. If the down lineman plays straight or goes outside, the offensive blocker is in perfect position to seal the linebacker. If the down lineman comes inside, the offensive lineman locks on him and drives him inside on a drive block.

We use a little different type of block when teaching the gap blocking. To block a gap, the first thing the blocker has to do is control his inside area. If I am gap blocking, I am blocking the first defender to my inside between me and the ball. The first thing I have to do is prevent penetration through the gap. The fastest way the blocker can cover the inside is to step down immediately. We don't aim at the hips. We take a lateral move. As I am taking a lateral move to the inside, I read the defender's charge. The first thing I want to do is to read the stance of the defender. If his head is down and his butt up, he probably is coming hard into the gap. If he is back in his stance, he is probably reading. As I lateral-step to the inside, and as the defender comes into my gap, I want to get the biggest piece of him as I can. If I get my head inside on him, that is great. If I don't, I take the biggest piece of him I can get. If he is reading, my next step is upfield. I try to get my hands inside and drive him down inside. If the defender loops into the face of the blocker, it is back to the base block.

The next type of block is the Hesitation Block. This is a technique used by the offensive guard to keep from getting picked off by a slanting defensive tackle when he is trying to block a linebacker. The offensive tackle blocks his man anywhere he wants to go. The guard steps to the defensive tackle and reads his movement. If the tackle is playing straight or going outside, the guard comes up and attacks the linebacker. If the tackle slants to the outside, the guard comes and attacks the linebacker. If the tackle slants to the inside, the guard reaches with his outside hand, puts it on the butt of the offensive tackle, pulls himself around and attacks the linebacker on his side of the line of scrimmage. If the linebacker is at his normal depth we use this technique. If he is on the line of scrimmage we go get him right now.

The last technique I want to show you is when two offensive linemen can block one gap control defender and linebacker when he shows. It is two linemen controlling the line of scrimmage and then blocking the linebacker later. The two linemen take a move so that they can control the gap area. We have an inside and outside control area. We can control the inside with the inside man coming off for the linebacker. Or we can control the line with the outside man coming off for the linebacker.

The next thing I am going to talk about is pass protection. We could spend all day here talking about 101 ways to pass block. You know what I want to do with the ball. I want to run that ball. I do not want to take away from my running game by spending a lot of time learning how to protect the passer. I had to find something that fits into my scheme that would allow me to become a great pass protector without taking away from my running game. We wanted our linemen to fire out but still stay under control. We wanted the linebackers and defensive backs to see run from our offensive line, even when we pass.

The first thing we teach our linemen in pass protection is how to read a rush from a defender. If he has his head down his rush will be hard and physical. If he raises up in the air with the body, his rush will be some kind of finesse move.

As soon as the lineman straightens his legs in pass protection he is dead. We eye the defender in the numbers. We want to know where the QB is going to set up. We want to know where the point of no return is. And, we want to stay between the defender and the passer. We must be patient, have good feet, and good initial movement.

Let me talk about four different sets we teach in our pass protection. This allows me to coach my players by the numbers so they know what I am talking about.

■ The "1 Set" is the Inside Blocking Technique. The key to this set is to keep the weight off the inside foot. I also want to maintain a power move position. That is a slight stagger in my feet with a good base. That allows me to shuffle down inside. The initial move is down inside, maintaining good weight distribution and a power position.

■ The "2 Set" is for a heads-up technique by the defender. It is like the "1 Set" in that my first responsibility is inside, but I don't step to the inside. I simply move my feet up and I am already in the proper position.

■ In the "3 Set" the responsibility is for the outside move. That is the reverse of the "1 Set." My weight distribution is on the inside and outside foot light.

■ The "4 Set" is for a wide charge from the defender. I want to take him on as close to the line of scrimmage as possible. We want to stay parallel with the line of scrimmage and take him on as quickly as we can. The weight has to be on the inside foot. We want to shuffle and take this move deep and out of the passing lane. If the defender comes inside, the blocker has his power move with the weight on the inside.

I don't like to lock up with a rusher. When we do that we tend to forget about our feet. When the rusher moves we tend to fall and try to drag him down. I want to lock out, recoil, and take him on again. That keeps my feet moving. You don't block a man with your hands and arms. You block him with your feet. You want to move your feet and legs and maintain your position.

When we set up we want the elbows in. We don't want the defender to touch our shoulders. We want our hands active enough to keep the defender's hands off our shoulders.

Now, what do you do with all of this material I have just covered? What I want you to do is go home and teach the techniques that fit into your system of offense. When you coach offense, you must know *why* something doesn't work. You can't grab-bag and try to find something that works. When the play breaks down, you have to know why so the next play can take advantage of what happened.

Chapter 6

OFFENSIVE LINE
TECHNIQUES AND DRILLS

By
Danny Hope
Purdue University
1998

I am going to talk a little about techniques and drills and how to transfer techniques onto the playing field. I would like to talk a little about philosophy. You must know where you are coming from to get where you want to go. You must have something to hang your hat on. With Coach Joe Tiller, our number 1 team goal was to have fun. It may sound elementary but it works for us at Purdue. We don't fear failure. Coach Tiller told me for most of his career he did not focus on having fun, but for the latter part of his career he wants to have fun first. It carries over into the attitude of the players as enthusiasm is contagious. Having fun is the philosophy our head coach hangs his hat on.

As an offensive line coach with Coach Howard Schnellenberger, I spent a lot of time teaching assignments on the football field. Coach Schnellenberger pulled me aside and told me that in order to be a good offensive line coach, I shouldn't hang my hat on being an assignment football coach. If I only teach assignments, there are a few things happening. One, I have too many plays, and I need to condense my schemes, or my players are stupid and I cannot teach. You don't want to focus only on assignments because the things that make a difference in offensive line play are technique and tempo. In practice if you are spending a lot of time on who a player is going to block, you are not watching what they are doing technique-wise and you are not pushing them to get away from the defense.

The philosophy I adopted in the last several years is to keep it simple, reduce the number of schemes, improve as a technique coach, and try to make a difference in the tempo. After every practice, I ask myself this question, "Did I make a difference in the technique or tempo of the practice?" Some days when I walk off the field I am a little disappointed in myself. Asking this question encourages me to assert myself from the start to the end of practice. To win on the offensive line, you need to practice technique and tempo.

When I coached the line at Louisville, Wyoming, Oklahoma, and Purdue this year, there were three elements I wanted the offensive linemen to hang their hats on. The number 1 fact with offensive linemen is "Want To." "Want To" is the overriding factor in how good a player is. Guys who are average athletes can be the best players, as they have the most heart. I have had great athletes who were average players because they have less heart. We try to emphasize "Want To" in our group and make it a part of us. You have to critique it and point it out on the field. When you are running sprints, you have to challenge the guys to be first and show the players how important "Want To" really is.

The second element that is important is "Tempo." Being politically correct we use the word "Vaginal" as an adjective. If you have a "Vaginal" offensive line, then there is a good chance you may be a "Vaginal" offensive line coach. Think about it. Now, the players they gave to you are not natural-born ass kickers. You have to take your guys and insist that they play aggressive. You must teach them how to be aggressive. We want that to be our trademark. The best compliment for an offensive line coach is to have another coach tell you this: "Damn, your guys play hard and your guys play really tough."

The tempo is very, very important to me. There are some things you can do in practice to make the linemen tough and more aggressive. In individual periods we spend a lot of that time working on individual drills. We try to go on a high tempo and try to get it on during that period. For example, every day we work on Cut Blocking. I like to start every day with that drill for a couple of reasons. I want to get the players running full speed, lunging forward, being reckless, and getting on the ground. A lot of times linemen are afraid to get on the ground. Every day for about 10 minutes, we work on running down the field sawing the defensive players down. It is a high-tempo-type drill.

Another thing we do every single day is "Boards and Bags." This is where the players are working on their footwork on the inside zone. They have to be very physical because we do not stop. We will go over that drill later, but it has to be a physical drill. A lot of people run the drill but they do not make the drill aggressive. We use "Boards and Bags" as an aggressive drill.

During the spring we do a lot of "Shoot Drills." For fear of injury, I don't do them during the season much. There seems to be a problem with offensive linemen now in that they do not want to put their face on anyone. In the pass protection, they put their hands in front of themselves. In the springtime, we want the guys to accelerate through the shoots against air. Then we put the offensive linemen against the linemen in the shoot. We do it in the spring, so in the season when we come off the ball and run the Inside Zone, our linemen are hitting as hard as they can. We do a lot of shoot work in the spring because we think it makes them aggressive and encourages them to go in and hit people with their faces.

We do a drill we call the "Fill Block" where a player works on stepping forward like a center if he as going to go back on somebody, or the tackle gapping down. We do a "Fill Drill" where we are firing off the ball with a point of aim where we are making contact with each other.

The tempo makes the difference in the offensive line. This year we had a player named Mark Fisher. He is an offensive line coach's dream. He was as tough as they come. He was such an aggressive player that he gave the other players someone to emulate.

The last element is the "Us" aspect. It is the Us or Togetherness as a group. This year I had a very efficient offensive line. Individually they were not outstanding players but worked well as a group. In order to have a cohesive offensive line, I think you have to give them something a little special. We will ask the line to do something extra as a team, whether it is sit-ups or pass sets. I am always trying to give them something extra to do together. Anytime you give them something extra to do that will bond them closer and the more they will feel special.

I think you are kidding yourself if you think you are just going to show up and coach. I think that is a crime in our profession today. For some coaches the only time they are around the players is when it is time to coach them on the field. Coaching requires more personal interaction with the players, especially when you have a large support staff, so when you have to get salty with them they know you love them and they can trust you. We hang our hat on the Want To, the Tempo, and the Us thing. If you do not do all three things you will not overachieve on the offensive line. You will not play well enough to win all of your games. The players you get on the offensive line are not good enough to play to their ability. They have to play above their ability. They need these three elements.

Let me cover the Stances. We do not spend a lot of time on stances. We vary our stances based on down and distance, whether or not the play is going to be a five-step drop or a third-and-long situation.

If you are going to put them in an up stance, they are going to be in an up stance. If it is third and 1 and you are going to run the ball and they have their butt up in the air, that is fine. It is when you don't want them to know if you are running or passing is when you have a problem with the stance. If you run the ball all of the time no one would have any problem with the stance because everyone would have their butts up in the air. The same is true if you throw the ball all of the time and you have your butt down all of the time.

We do a drill that we call "Run or Pass—Check-With-Me." We run this drill during the off-season. The linemen get in their stance and wait for a RUN or PASS call and then shift their weight forward. If it is a pass they shift the weight back. We work on shifting their weight without adjusting their hands. We do not worry on how high or low their hips are. We tell them we are going to run right or pass right. We get them down in their stance and tell them "SET." I will call out "Pass Right" and on Hut they have to get their hands up and boom, they have to get over here and set up for a pass. If I call Run Right they have to do run steps when I call "SET." We work on an Up Stance and we do not give a damn if they know we are going to throw the ball. Then we will get in a three-point stance and we do not care if they know we are going to run the ball. The rest of the time we are in a balanced stance. We try to shift our weight around a little without changing our hand placement on the ground.

I think you have to work on stance and starts a lot during the off-season. During the season you want to work on football. You can't spend half of your time working on stance during the season. The linemen must be disciplined enough to get together and go outside and work on their stance on their own. On Thursdays and Fridays during the season when we do not practice as much, I try to take the first five minutes of individual work to get them back into a regular stance. Typically, as the season progresses, their stances get sloppier. I see them in the film and I can't believe some of the players in their stances. We want to prevent bad habits.

I want to talk about Fill Blocking. Some of you may call it Gap Down Blocking. If you want to make an offensive line coach nervous just ask him how to Gap Block down. He is nervous because he can never be right. The best way to block a gap block, where you can cut off protection, and also the back door, is to take the inside foot and step at the defender's far foot. That is your point of aim. You have to gain ground or the defender will get penetration. So, if I am going to gap block down on my inside, I put the weight on my outside foot, and I push with my outside foot and step toward his far foot and try to put my face in the V of the defender's neck. I try to drive his butt out of there.

When we teach the basic gap block, we will come out with two lines of defensive players. We have one line of offensive players. We have the defensive line get down first. Then we have the offensive blocker line up. We can gap block left or right. You can stand behind the blocker to see that he is right with his technique. You have to watch his feet. We always have the defensive players line up first in order to give you a true look. We work either gap blocking to the left or right. We make the guy standing behind the blocker watch to make sure he sees what is going on and that he is right with the technique. If you don't do a lot of filling or gap blocking, it is still a good drill to teach you to push off as you step. I have a tape here that will shows our center's gap blocking.

Gap block drill and technique. Step at the defender's far foot with your inside foot. Put your face in the V of defender's neck. The offensive man can gap block in either direction. Both defenders penetrate with movement by the offensive lineman.

The center must be aggressive and obtain his block in the trap block in gap blocking.

When we go out in the pre-game warm-up before a game there are several different drills we do. One of them is gap block.

Another drill we use is pass protection on a sled. I believe there are two reasons why you get beat on pass protection. Take missed assignments and players not getting off on the snap, and this is what we find:

1) You get outside your center of gravity.

2) You set up in the wrong place.

All the drills we use in season and out of season as far as pass protection goes are things that are going to help you get out of your stance and maintain your center of gravity. We choreograph the sets based on the steps of the quarterback's drop and the alignment of the defender.

I want to get into the drills that help us keep our center of gravity. In order to keep their center of gravity, we tell our linemen this: We want them to imagine they have a seven-foot steel rod stuck in the top of their head. Then we run the rod down the player's body. He has two feet of the rod sticking from his head. If we would stand behind the player we would see his center of gravity can be maintained by keeping the bar vertical. It should be straight up and down.

Another drill we have is a sled drill where we ask them to change direction and do some things on the sled. We think this drill helps them with their pass protection techniques and it also helps to keep their center of gravity on blocks. We do this drill every day.

We have them tea bag and bend. We have them bend the knees and keep their heels on the ground as well as their butt to the grass. We call that tea bagging. You have to keep the heels flat on the ground. Then we work on sitting down in the sweet spot in a position where we feel comfortable to take on the defender. We work on stabbing the bag, straight line shots, from our breast to their breast. We emphasize taking the triceps and squeezing the front of your rib cage so the elbows are not dropping before you stab. This means our hands get on the defender faster. We ask them to lock the bag out, to sit down and separate, and to squeeze the edge of the bag.

We run the Inside Zone Play. It is our 34 and 35 Sprint. We use the Board and Bag Drills to help up with these plays. I really want you to see this drill first. When we line up on the line of scrimmage we want our helmet on the bottom of the center's numbers. That is how deep we have our offensive linemen off the ball. The rule is that they have to break the center's hip. If you line up at the center's numbers you are about as close as you can be. We want them back off the ball so they can get over in front of the defender before he knocks the crap out of them. They have to get over on the defender at their point of aim. If you crowd the ball, contact is made before the blocker can get over on the defender. When we are working on our Drive Block, which we used on our Inside Zone play, we give the linemen a point of aim. We tell them to take their nose and split the defender's sternum at the outside numbers. We want his inside foot slightly inside the defender's inside foot. That is the fit that we want. We feel if we can get back off the ball we can get over in position to get our face on the defender. We feel the contact will happen on the second step. So, when we do Boards and Bags we back them off just enough to make the drill effective. We tell the bag holder to move forward. That is what the defense does. We do not want the bag holder to stand back and let the blocker drive him 15 yards off the ball. We want the blocker to go over and then up. The defender with the bag steps forward and jams the bag into the blocker as hard as he can. The last time we played, the defense was coming across the line as hard as they could. So we want the man with the bag doing the same thing. If the man holding the bag does not make it an aggressive drill we will take the bag away from him and make it live for him. The guy holding the bag is the key to the drill. The blocker does not get anything out of the drill if the defender does not do the drill right. This is a good assessment of what we are going to get.

BOARD AND BAG DRILL VS. HEAD-UP DEFENDER

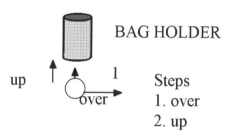

BAG HOLDER

up   over   1   Steps
1. over
2. up

We have established the fact that contact will take place on the second step. We have backed the offensive man off the ball. We want them to dip the shoulders as they take that first step to get their pads low. We emphasize this a lot but you do not see them dropping down very much, but we do not see them raising up a lot. The first step, which we call the Set Step, is the one that gets them over. We want them to lower their pads. If they can lower the pads one inch instead of raising them by three inches that is four inches of leverage. That is a lot of leverage.

Next we offset the board and block at an angle. This would be a right guard on a 3 Technique defender, or it could be a tackle on a 5 Technique, or an end on a 9 Technique. Now, for the blocker to get his face outside and up into the defender's numbers he has to move over and back a little. We take a bucket or drop-step. We bucket-step gaining width and depth. Then we step up. We offset the board in order to emulate the defender lining up off the outside shoulder of the lineman.

VS. OUTSIDE ALIGNMENT

Steps
1. Bucket w/ width & depth
2. up

We do a lot of work with Boards and Bags. We work on the bags both right and left.

The next drills are the Cut Drills. I know you cannot cut in high school. However, there is some carryover in this drill. We are cutting the linebacker in this drill. We offset him so it is more like a game situation.

LINEBACKER CUT OR CLIMB DRILL

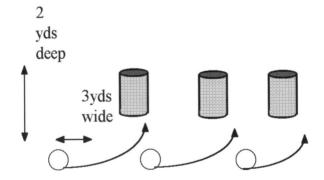

We tell the blocker to get on top of the defender. We want to take the arm and rip it through the crotch of the linebacker. We want the shoulder pads coming up. We want to get as close to the defender as possible. We throw off the outside foot. We want to get on top of the man before we throw. We tell them to run to their legs and get on top of them before we throw. A coaching point is this: When we land on the ground we get up running. We do not lay on the ground. We do this for two reasons. One, we can continue to tie the man up. Second, we can get downfield and get another man.

We use our Reach Block on our Outside Zone Plays, which are our 38 and 39 Sprint. We also use the block on the Toss Play. The thing on the Reach Block is what you teach as the point of aim and what you are making contact with. We want to take our backside pad and get it on the defender's outside pad. A lot of people teach the block by telling the blocker to take his face and get it on the outside of the numbers. By teaching the block by getting the backside pad on his outside pad I think two things happen for you:

1) If I am trying to reach a real wide man and I am trying to get my backside pad on his outside pad it will usually take care of where my feet should go in order for me to get the angle on the defender. You do not have to teach a lot of lead step footwork if you are teaching backside pad on outside pad. They will step wide if they do this.

2) If I get my backside pad on the defender's outside pad the defender has to fight through my neck and head in order to get to the ball carrier. If we just put our nose on him he can slip off and get to the play. When we teach the Reach Block we want that backside pad on the outside pad. We try not to cross over for our second step. We do not teach it but it happens at times. We teach them on the Reach Block to never step past their midline. We want them to get their foot down and never step over the midline. We teach them to take a big drop step, a bucket step, and I want to make sure we are getting depth and width. We want the back pad on the outside pad. Once I get that leverage it is critical that I get heavy with my outside arm and then fight like hell to get North and South.

REACH BLOCK DRILL

Reach Block Technique

BS
pad

E to defenders
outside pad

Bucket step with
width and depth

Another drill I picked up from a former Illinois coach is very helpful in teaching this block. We take two offensive linemen and line them head up on each other. We have both offensive linemen try to reach each other at the same time. They try to get their backside pad on the outside pad of the other man. This is a great drill. The man that gets off the ball first has the advantage. They are both doing the same drill and they are using the same technique. They really work on getting off on the snap count. It teaches the blockers to fight like hell to get to the outside on the Reach Block. They have to get their feet moving and they have to stay up on the man. This has been a good drill for us, especially for our centers who have to do a lot of reach blocking. Also, it has helped our tight ends and our tackles on the open side. When you are talking about Reach Blocking the vertical alignment is critical. We review this all of the time. We want the helmet on the center's bottom part of his numbers. By halftime the officials should come over on the sideline and tell us that we have to move our linemen up on the line more.

When we run our Outside Zone Plays, 38 and 39 Sprint, we break into two parts. We have two linemen on offense. We have an offensive tackle that is covered and a guard that is uncovered.

When we teach the Outside Zone we teach it as covered or uncovered techniques. If I am the guard and we are running the Outside

Zone play, and the tackle is covered, then the guard is the uncovered man. The guard will take the defender if he goes inside. We tell the covered man this. If the man is heads up, we want the tackle to over reach and rip pad under pad and try to slow the man down a little for the backside guard. The closer the linebacker gets to the play, the wider you must lead. If a man is head up or on the inside eye, we expect that blocker to be the one who comes off on the linebacker.

When you are the uncovered man, some people call them the trail man, but we call them the short puller. The reason for this is because the technique we are using is a short pull technique. There are three steps he must use on this technique. The first thing he must do is to open his hips up and point my nose toward the boundary. He must open up all the way. They must be able to go off the tail of the cover man. If they do not open up enough it is hard to get the head across the bow if the defender pinches.

The second step is to go for the outside number of the defender. He has to be looking for that aiming point.

The third step is an action. If I see his outside number, one of two things happens. Either he takes him over and keeps his head across the bow, or he turns it up at the linebacker.

Chapter 7

TEACHING THE BASIC DRIVE BLOCK

By
Dave Magazu
University of Kentucky
1996

I am going to be talking about Offensive Line Play at the University of Kentucky. First I will cover the Teaching Progression of the Base Block. Next I will take you through a Chute Progression. Then I will talk about a Horn Block and a Gap Block. These are basically Man Blocks that we use in our Zone Blocking Scheme. We call it our Inside Zone and our Outside Zone Plays, and we incorporated some Man Schemes depending on the defense.

At the University of Kentucky we do not have a play in our scheme where we use a Base Block. However, the Base Block is the most important block that we teach, and it is the first block that we teach. All of the aspects of the Base Block are involved in each block that we use. All of the techniques that we use when we teach the Base Block will carry over into the other blocks, as far as hat placement, hand placement, footwork, and how you get into the block. Every single block needs to have an aiming point, and you need the footwork that allows you to get into your aiming point. Once you get into your aiming point everything turns into the Base Block. To say we come out and Base Block at the point of attack is not true. We just do not do a lot of that.

When we talk about Base Blocking or any form of blocking, we are talking about Option Blocking. We really do not try to swing our rear end one way or the other. We try to stay square on most of our blocks. The teaching progression is to teach the Base Block first and then have that carry over to all of our other blocks. We will teach the Base Block in the reverse order. The only equipment we use will be

59

Chutes. Also, we use a board that is beveled on the side, and is 12 feet long.

BLOCKING CHUTE—DIMENSIONS
   TOP—59 X 70
   BOTTOM—54
   FRONT—46
   BACK—58

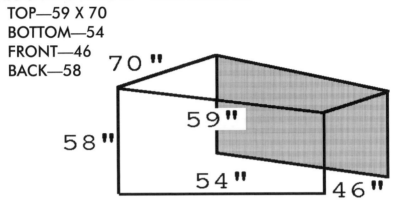

We have two points that we stress at Kentucky as far as Offensive Line Play. First, we will be the toughest line on the field. Second, we will never quit on a block any time during the game. There are a lot of techniques to be concerned with in coaching offensive linemen.

TEACHING PROGRESSION—BASE BLOCK
We believe that the Base Block is the most important block of an offensive lineman. This is used when blocking at the point of attack. The objective is to get movement, option blocking the defender the way he wishes to go. You must maintain contact, allowing the runner to option run defenders.

Following is the sequence of how we teach this Drive Block. First we teach stance and start, then sequences are taught in the reverse order to ensure the athlete experiences the perfect block.

FIRST PHASE
STANCE/START—LINEMAN STANCE
■ Feet

   — Good base—at least armpit-width but never wider than your shoulders.

   — Toes in—heels out (depends upon technique being used).

   — Feet—toes to instep or toe-to-heel relationship.

■ Power-Producing Angles

— Weight on the inside balls of the feet.

— Knees in and over the ankles.

— Want "Z" in the knees.

— The power-producing angles are created by the bend in the ankle and knee joints.

■ Down Hand

— Placed slightly inside the rear foot.

— Extended comfortably from the shoulder.

— Reach out far enough to create a balanced stance, 60 percent forward, 40 percent back.

— Five fingertips on ground.

■ Off Hand

— Wrist to the side of the knee.

— Make a light fist with hand.

■ Shoulder—parallel to the LOS.

■ Back—parallel to the ground.

■ Tail—slightly higher than the shoulders.

■ Head

— Cocked back slightly.

— In a "Bull" neck position.

— See feet of defender.

I think stance is important. It does not matter what position you coach in football; a coach has to emphasize stance every day and on every play. It has to happen automatically. We spend a lot of time with this every day. We believe in a stance where you are going to be bunched up. The players will feel a little uncomfortable at first. We do not want them to overextend. I still cannot figure out why the pro players get their legs spread so far apart. We are just the opposite of that type of stance. We start off toe to instep. We never let them get more than toe to heel. The reason we do this is because we are going to be pulling and we have a Horn Technique, and we have to set up to pass block. If we have our feet under us we can go in either direction.

The next phase is the Start. Every coach in America yells at his players, "We must stay low. We must come out of our stance low and we play with leverage." How do you get your players to do this? It is not bending at the waist. It is bending at the knees. Linemen must have the flexibility to bend at the knees. If you come and watch us practice you will hear me tell our linemen on their first step to pick their foot up and set it back down where they start from. They can't do that. I am trying to get them to pick up that first step and try to put it back where they started. They will only take a three- to six-inch step. If we tell them to take a six-inch step they step out 12 to 18 inches. We want a short step on the start. We spend a lot of time on this phase.

LINEMAN START

- Initial movement must be forward, not up.

- Like a sprinter going out of the blocks, you are trying to create FORCE.

- Step with appropriate foot when firing out to block:
    - Man Over—drive off the up foot and step with the rear foot.

    - Man Either Side—step with the foot nearest him.

- Coaching Points—Rear Foot Lead.
    - Mentally shift the weight to the push foot and step with your rear foot.

    - One-step drill:

- First step should be three-inch step out and slightly up, attacking the LOS.

- The knee of the up foot should point toward the ground (it should roll over the toe of the up foot).

- Arm action—like a sprinter coming out.

- Back flat—chest on the thigh.

- Bull your neck—sight your target.
    - Follow up quickly with second and third steps.

    - Stay low and maintain lift leverage.

- Coaching Points—Up Foot Lead
    - Mentally shift the weight to the push foot and step with the up foot.

— One-Step Drill—First step should be three-inch step out and slightly up attacking the line of scrimmage.

SECOND PHASE—FIT POSITION

The second phase is the FIT POSITION. We are still talking about the Base Block. The purpose is to show the blocker the ideal blocking position utilizing the power-producing angles.

FIT POSITION

■ We must put the defender in a challenging position and have the offensive blocker fit into him.

■ Offensive Blocker

— Feet are in a toe-instep relationship (stance).

— Good bend in knees—create power-producing angles.

— Knees in over the ankles.

— Butt down.

— Back arched.

— Good bull neck.

— Eyes in the solar plexus of the defender.

— Arms are in a blocking position, elbow points must break the plane of your hips, heels of the hands at the bottom of the defender's breastplate, forming a triangle with hairline and both fists (thumbs up/fingers through).

■ Defender—Challenge Position

— Feet slightly staggered—up foot at the edge of the board.

— Hold blocker under the arm.

— Give resistance.

THIRD PHASE—FOLLOW-THROUGH

The purpose is to have the player experience an ideal block. To teach the proper use of leverage, the hip roll, the acceleration of the feet, and the maintenance of a block.

■ The offensive blocker will align in a fit position, toes at the end of the board.

■ The defender will be in a challenging position holding the blocker in place. (The defender must give steady resistance.)

■ Walking Down The Board

— The blocker will walk the defender down the board with "a bulled" neck, power-producing angles and feeling pressure at the small of his back; never raise up.

— Walk the defender off the board, driving knees into the ground. Blocker's weight should be on the instep of each foot. (Do not be up on your toes!)

■ Hip Roll

— The blocker will roll his hips and accelerate his feet. When executing a block, he will make contact and have a stale-mate—in order to get movement, the blocker must roll his hips and accelerate his feet to dominate a defender.

— Hip roll is the underneath action—the snapping of your knees straight out and the shooting of your hips through.

— The feet should be underneath your shoulder pads to guard against overextension.

■ Hold

— Halfway down the board, on the command "Hold," the blockers will stop.

— Check the position of the blocker.

FOURTH PHASE—CONTACT

Of all of the phases we do, the players struggle on this more than on any of the others. The purpose is to teach the contact phase of the drive block technique. Emphasize arm and timing of the pop.

■ Offensive blocker is in a down position and situates himself one step from the defender.

■ The defensive man will assume a challenging position.

■ The defender should be in a good two-point stance, bending his knees as much as possible with his chest out and head tucked.

■ He will catch the blocker rather than deliver a lick.

■ The offensive blocker takes only one step, jolting the defender backward.

■ Concentrate on ripping the arms and taking short, powerful steps.

■ Follow through by driving the defender off the board.

FIFTH PHASE—HIT AND DRIVE

The purpose of the drill is to put all aspects of the Drive Block together. We start at the back end of the Chute and work under it with the blockers. We do this every Tuesday and Wednesday when we are in pads. You can set the tempo of the drill.

■ Align the offensive blocker in a three-point stance, a foot away from the defender, toes at the end of the board.

■ To start, the defender will be in a two-point stance; as the drill progresses, he will move to a three-point stance without the boards.

■ The offensive blocker will explode out of his stance and drive a defender down the board. Emphasize good base and acceleration of the feet.

■ As the drill progresses, vary the distance between the blocker and the defender to aid in the development of a rhythm of blocking a defender at varied distances away.

■ Use TWO-WHISTLE DRILL—First whistle to check body position; second whistle to release athlete from the drill.

SIXTH PHASE—SECOND EFFORT

The purpose is to teach the blocker to maintain contact when the defender is spinning out or disengaging the blocker.

■ The coach will give the defender a direction to spin.

■ When the defender reaches the end of the board, he will sprint out of the block in direction indicated by the coach on the second whistle.

■ The blocker must step with the near foot in the direction of the spin, aggressively attacking the defender.

■ Never cross your feet or kick your heels together. You must maintain a good base.

SEVENTH PHASE —VS. SHADE ALIGNMENTS

The purpose is to teach the drive block on opponents aligned in shaded or offset alignments.

■ Same as hit-and-drive phase except we start from position with inside foot on outside of board.

■ First step must be perfect to get to solar plexus of defender. Second step must be upfield, maintaining a good base.

■ Practice inside-to-outside shades of offensive blocker.

The aiming point on the Base Block is through the bottom of the numbers. That is where we want to form that triangle I talked about earlier. When you go through blocking drills you must tell the blocker where his aiming point is. We take the premise of stepping to the alignment and incorporate that into all of our Zone Blocking.

Next I want to cover the HORN BLOCK. Some people call it a Fold Block. This block is on the front side of a play and it can turn into a part of our Zone Scheme. The purpose of the Horn Block is to enable an offensive lineman to block linebackers going under or around the blocker to his outside. (The technique will vary according to the play.)

A Man Horn Block locks up a horn person on the linebacker and another offensive lineman on the defensive down lineman. It enables a lineman to go around or under a block to block a linebacker.

- Bucket step with depth, crossover (or hop) to stay square. Keep your toes pointed upfield.

- Keep shoulders square and read the defensive tackle.

- If tackle plays straight or outside, take easiest course to linebacker.

- If tackle comes inside, release around drive block for linebacker.

- Sustain contact, smother linebacker.

- Man Horn—Guard on linebacker all the way, through or around.

- Zone Horn—Guard blinks tackle for slant move. No slant, block linebacker through or around.

MAN HORN

 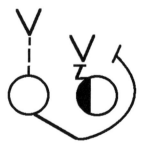

ZONE HORN

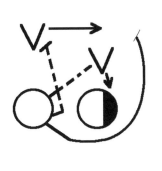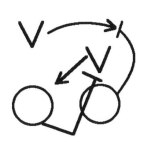

Now I want to talk about the Gap Block. We are going to put this into our Zone Scheme. We will coordinate the Gap Block with the Man Horn Block.

GAP BLOCK

The purpose of this block is to be able to block a defender to our inside gap, stopping all penetration at the point of attack (man blocking). Coaching points include the following:

■ Take a flat step to the inside. Use the defender's hands as an aiming point (three- to six-inch step).

■ Freeze the second step until you read the reaction of the defender.

■ If the defender tries to penetrate across the line of scrimmage, pivot and bring your outside foot across and shoulder block the defender's hip. Rip your outside arm and try to punch the defender's hip and work to his armpit.

■ If the defender starts to work across your face, step straight upfield on your second step and base block his outside number.

■ Stay up on the block—it is not a scramble.

INSIDE ZONE BLOCKING

Purpose: this is one of our basic blocking schemes. Our approach to zone blocking is to come off on the down defender with two blockers on one defender to get maximum push off the LOS, providing a pocket for the ball carrier to run into. We want to knock the first level defenders into the linebackers. At the second level (depth of the linebacker), we either push the first level defender into the linebacker, or the blocker to the linebacker side comes off on him. This play attacks the first down defender from the guard to the outside. The back plays a major role in the success of this play. He must run up behind the zone block on the first level defender before making his break to daylight. If he makes his cut too early, the linebacker flows too fast and the come-off blocker can't get him blocked. The key is for the back to run up behind the zone and then explode into a seam with power. Hold the linebackers in there.

Let me go over the coaching points. First is the lead blocker. The lead blocker comes off with power and quickness, aiming to a point that puts his hat on the outside hip of the first level defender. The blocker must stay low with a flat-level back and good base during this come-off. Against a wide-aligned defender, the blocker can use a flat or bucket step depending on the defender's width. The path established by this come-off is the lead blocker's TRACK. He must fight to stay square on the TRACK throughout the block.

Unless he has a Run-Through, the trail blocker will be joining the lead blocker at this point, helping him knock the first level defender off the line of scrimmage into the second level. The lead blocker must have his head and eyes up looking for the linebacker to show up on his side. If he shows up, the lead blocker comes off square on him. Patience is the key to coming off on the linebacker. If the blocker comes off too early, we won't get the necessary push on the first level defender. Let the RB bring the linebacker to you.

If the first level defender slants inside, the lead blocker stays on the TRACK, immediately looking for and blocking the linebacker scraping off the slant man's hips. Don't overrun the scraper; be under control—stay square. If he is frozen inside, turn inside and wall him off.

If the down man plays into the path of the lead blocker, the blocker has him by himself. He stays square with the track working the defender off the line of scrimmage. He can't be flattened; he wants to stay square and STRETCH the defender to the outside. A wide-aligned defender will most likely widen when the blocker bucket-steps.

Let me go over the Trail Blocker. The trail blocker will use a Horn technique taking a bucket step with the foot nearest the lead blocker. He drops this foot back and to the outside, pointing the toe down the TRACK. It is important to get the shoulders perpendicular to the BUCKET STEP—get in position to look down the TRACK. Stay low and have good vision; you must read the actions of the defenders while bucket-stepping.

The first threat the trail blocker could have is the linebacker RUN-THROUGH. A presnap read can help establish the run-through possibility. If the linebacker is close and up on his toes leaning toward the line of scrimmage, there is a good chance for the run-through. The deeper he aligns, the less chance there is. If the run-through develops, drive off the bucket-step foot and snap your shoulders off upfield and take on the linebacker square.

The next threat to the trail blocker is for the first level defender to slant toward him. If this occurs, the blocker drives off the bucket step and shoulder spears the slant man with his hat to the play side.

If there is no run-through or slant threat, the trail blocker drives off the bucket-step foot on a track, which puts his hat on the near hip of the first level defender. If the defender is playing tough into the lead blocker, the trail blocker shoulder spears, arm rolls, lifts, and drives him down the track to the second level. It is important to stay square running along the TRACK.

During this maneuver, the blocker's head and eyes must be up so he can keep vision on the linebacker. When reaching the linebacker's depth, with the linebacker still on his side of the block, the trail blocker comes off square into the linebacker. If the linebacker flows behind or across the block on the first level defender, the trail blocker concentrates all his attention and force to driving him down the track.

If the down defender stretches the lead blocker, the trail blocker should stay square on his track to the linebacker. Front up the linebacker, keeping shoulders square.

A wide-aligned first level defender is already stretched and the trail blocker continues off the bucket step along the track to the linebacker.

When the linebacker aligns in an UP POSITION, the run-through has been committed. The trail blocker has his man and comes directly off the ball on his outside number.

The techniques for the back side of the inside ZONE are basically the same as the front side. The only technique change is that the TRACK ANGLE is sharper. The lead blocker takes off on a track with half of his shoulder pad on the first level defender's play-side hip. The trail blocker comes off on a track, which would put him through the middle of the first-level defender's initial alignment.

This technique will vary according to the linebacker's alignment. The lead blocker will use more of a rip technique. The tighter the linebacker is to the play, the thinner the lead blocker is; therefore, the more the aiming point of the trail blocker will change. The trail blocker may go from the defender's middle to far number to armpit.

Let me go over some blocking schemes on the Inside Zone.

INSIDE ZONE VS. 5-2

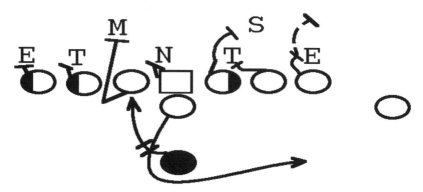

INSIDE ZONE VS. 4-3

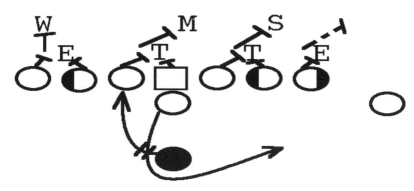

INSIDE ZONE VS. 4-3

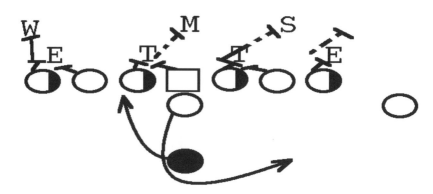

Very quickly let me get to the Outside Zone Blocking. Coaching Points on the Lead Block include the following: The lead blocker will use a rip technique or a lead technique (depending on position) on outside ZONE. He is trying to miss the first-level defender by ripping under him to the side of the play; he then works for a wall-off position on the linebacker. He releases on a TRACK ANGLE that is outside the first-level defender to the side of the play. If he makes it through, he works upfield and backside to wall the linebacker. He must not overrun the linebacker. He should have his head and eyes up looking for him immediately as he clears the down defender. He should be especially alert if he feels the first-level man slanting away.

If, as the lead blocker releases, the first-level defender works into him tough, he must work hard to redirect his track upfield. Second effort is important here to keep the defender from playing across the blocker's head. If the blocker will keep driving to get through, he will cut off the first-level defender. If the linebacker is up on the trail blocker or in a tight run-through position, the lead blocker takes a cutoff angle on the man.

The trail blocker will use a horn technique by taking a deep bucket step, reading the defenders. If he gets early linebacker run-through, he turns up on him and wheels him away from the play.

If the down lineman slants to the trail blocker, he turns upon the slant man and wheels him away from the play. If the slant man is penetrating deep, push him by and release upfield to wall the next defender.

If there is no run-through or slant at the trail blocker, he drives off the bucket-step foot on a deep pulling path, running a course that would allow him to get his hat on the far knee of the first-level defender. As the lead blocker starts to clear the defender, the trail blocker drives his upfield shoulder stabbing the play-side leg. On contact, he drives up the field hard with second effort, wheeling him inside.

If the lead blocker is stretched, the trail blocker will try to horn around the stretch to the linebacker. As the trail blocker starts his horn, he must get his depth and width. As he attacks the line of scrimmage it is very important for him to keep his shoulders square and attack the linebacker's outside number. If the down lineman stretches too far, the trail blocker must get inside the stretch and run the linebacker by the play.

On the outside zone plays, don't be afraid to cut the defense. Let me cover some blocking schemes on the Outside Zone Play.

OUTSIDE ZONE VS. 5-2

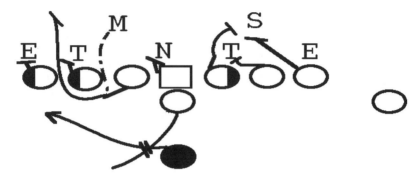

OUTSIDE ZONE VS. 4-3

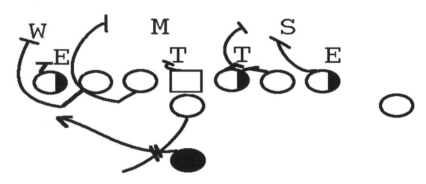

OUTSIDE ZONE VS. 4-3

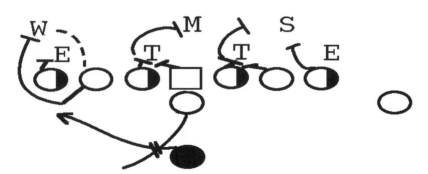

I will talk about our Inside Zone Play, and look at the Outside Zone Play. You will see the play from the wide angle first, and then you will see the tight copy.

OUTSIDE ZONE VS. 4-3

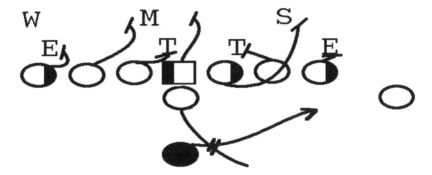

OUTSIDE ZONE VS. 5-2

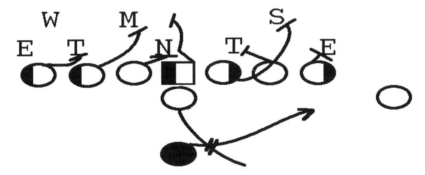

Chapter 8

OFFENSIVE LINE DRILLS AND TECHNIQUES

By
Steve Marshall
UCLA
1996

Every place I've ever been we have been kind of a multiple offense. What I'm going to do today is try to give you what I teach our offensive line when we talk about multiplicity of offense. The offensive coordinator wants to get into a multitude of sets and have a lot of different ways to do it. For the offensive line it is important to have a simple and direct way to teach a lot of things.

I have not been an option-type coach. What happens to the offensive line when you do not run the option is that you see a lot of defensive fronts because the defense doesn't have to play option responsibility. I guess some of this is theory, but I like to teach our offensive line a lot of different things and group them into packages.

The biggest thing in coaching the offensive line is to put it into an easy form to learn. The offensive linemen must learn to come up to the ball and get after somebody's tail. They don't need to worry about what to do. They need to focus on how to do it. We don't want those linemen thinking at the line of scrimmage. We want them to have a great attitude about coming off the ball and killing somebody. Offensive line coaches are the worst at this. They spend too much time with perfect footwork, hat placement, and things like that. Those things are not possible on every play. If you give them a base to understand what the play is and what you are trying to accomplish, then you have a chance.

There are three ways that we teach blocking schemes. I break down the plays that we want to run into three categories. The first group is MAN BLOCKING. An example of that would be numbering the defensive players. In an odd front defense, the noseguard is 0, the line-backer is 1, defensive tackle is 2, and so forth. From there we tell the center to block 0, the guard 1, the tackle 2, and the tight end 3. If I say FAN it means the guard blocks 1 on the line and the tackle blocks 2 on the line. That is how we would block MAN.

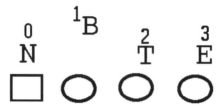

The second thing we have is a package of ZONE PLAYS. The base rule is an "ON DOWN LINEMAN" or an "OVER LINEBACKER." This means if the lineman has a down lineman ON him he blocks him. If he doesn't he finds the nearest linebacker OVER him. He is blocking an area scheme. There are all kinds of names for these techniques. Scoop blocking is zone blocking. The Power Slip is zone blocking. Linemen must have the concept of what they are doing.

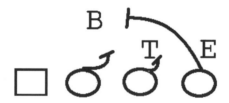

The third one I want to get into is my favorite. This is the COMBINA-TION BLOCK. It is a combination of man and zone blocking. The Counter Gap play is an example of this. We have some guys blocking zone and others are blocking man. Everybody has his own terms. What I'm going to use are the terms I know. The call-side guard and tackle are blocking area. But they are blocking the man within the area. The call-side tackle's rule is 5, 4, 3, 2, technique to the back-side linebacker. The call-side guard's rule is 3, 2, technique to the backside linebacker. The call-side guard and tackle step with their inside foot and take anything that comes all the way to the backside linebacker. I call it POP AND TURN.

The call-side guard steps inside protecting the A Gap area. The call-side tackle does the same thing to the B Gap. On the call side on a combination block, the guard and tackle know they are working in tandem. In this defense there is no 5 technique, but there is a 3 technique. They come off and the 3 technique goes outside. The tackle and guard pick that man up in tandem. The guard knows he is going to the backside linebacker at the proper time. This is an example of COMBINATION BLOCKING.

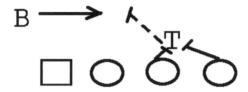

The offensive linemen within these three concepts should know how to handle everything we do. This does not include option blocking because that is a different set of rules. You could do some of these things in the option scheme, but there are different rules for most of it. There are different blocking techniques, but the base rules come from these three packages.

What I want to do is take one play step by step, the way we do it and how we teach it. The play that I want to use, because I think it is the ultimate smash-mouth play, is the Counter Trap. The Washington Redskins ran it and made it popular. This is the NCAA Run. Everybody has this play with the pass and naked play off it. It is kind of like a package within itself. In a single season we will run this play out of 10 to 15 different formations and 10 to 15 different ways. The concept for the big old meatheads up front never changes. I'll put up three different defenses and three different offensive sets.

I'm going to take you through our base rules of DOWN AND AROUND. I'll draw this first one up against a 40 defensive look from a Pro Set Weak for the offense. The tight end has three different things he could do. We sometimes go into a game with three different ways to block the same play. The defense gets pretty smart and reacts to the way an offense blocks. You can't do the same thing over and over again and expect the play to go consistently. For the teaching, I'll go through the different ways for you. The tight end's base rule is 7, 5, 4, 3, 2, to backside linebacker. In this defense he has no 7, 5, or 4 technique, he goes to the backside linebacker. This is called a CRAM IT technique. That means he is going inside regardless of alignment. He steps with his inside foot and forces his outside shoulder across the 6 technique. If the 6 technique comes inside, he takes him down with his zone principle. He gets his inside foot on the ground and blows through the outside hip of the tackle straight up the field for the backside linebacker. We tell him as he passes level 1 he gets vertical, but his eyes are on the back side. The coaching point is to never let anything cross his face. If anything crosses his face, he eats it up.

The defensive end will adjust to the inside move of the tight end and not let him inside. If he does that, the play is gone. We go to an influence scheme next for the tight end. We can SLAM INFLUENCE or just RELEASE. I like the Slam Influence. The tight end steps and targets the outside number of the defensive end as a landmark. The goal of the tight end is to make the defensive end widen. The ball is going inside the end. The tight end slam releases to the strong safety, outside linebacker, or whoever is out there, by blocking the defensive end for a moment and releasing him.

The tight end can also free release and block number 4 on the outside. The number 1 goal of the tailback is to cram the ball in the C Gap area.

The tackle's rule is 5, 4, 3, 2, to backside linebacker. There is no 5 or 4 technique in this defense. But there is a 3 technique. The onside guard has a 3, 2, 1, 0, to backside linebacker. The tackle and guard know they are working in combination on the 3 technique to the backside linebacker on level 2. A key coaching point here is to always take care of level 1. We want to take the 3 technique for the ride of his life. When I was at the University of Louisville we said knock his butt off the ball. Now that I'm at UCLA, an academic school, it is called a vertical push.

We want the 3 technique going backward, not down the line. The technique depends on whether you are the tackle or the guard. We recruit linemen. We don't recruit a left tackle. We recruit linemen, and they play all the positions. The guard knows he has the 3 technique. We want the guard to step with his inside foot, but he has to step relative to his technique.

The guard makes a call to the tackle. We use calls to communicate. You can use anything that you want as a call. Sometimes it is just as easy to say, "Partner, me and you are going to block the crap out of this guy." Whatever fits for you is the best way to do it. At some other places, I've had to have a call for everything.

We tell the lineman to take a PUNCH STEP. That means stick the foot into the ground so you have a base. The tackle has to step inside relative to the 3 technique. That means he has to step hard inside, or what we call a LATERAL PUNCH STEP. They are sticking their feet in the ground to block the 3 technique, but their eyes are backside on the linebacker. The guard is stepping and sticking the 3 technique on the inside half. The tackle sticks the 3 technique and he knows, since he is outside, he has the leverage on the 3 technique and linebacker. He has to maintain that leverage because the ball is going outside him in the C Gap. Since the tackle has leverage already, he uses both his hands to control the tackle. The guard has to see the backside linebacker and see his alignment. If the guard and tackle take the 3 technique for the ride of his life and let the linebacker run underneath them, we haven't accomplished a thing. The guard has to look at the alignment of the linebacker to see if he is normal or less than normal. Normal at Tennessee is 6 yards deep, running downhill. Normal at Washington is 2 yards deep. For the sake of this lecture, let's say the linebacker is shallow or less than normal. If that is the case, the guard is a one-hand player. All we are telling the guard is not to stick the inside hand into the 3 technique. We are two-on-one with the tackle, so we have to win. If the linebacker comes inside the guard he cannot physically turn his shoulder if he has stuck his inside hand into the 3 technique's body. If he sticks only his outside hand on the 3 technique, he has the ability to come off for the linebacker if he should run under the double team. If the linebacker plays the play normal and comes over the top of the double team, the guard gets his second hand on the 3 technique, takes him, and the tackle comes off for the linebacker. The guard has to have the feet of a burglar to hang on with one hand until that linebacker has committed to going across the double team. This technique could be the tight end-tackle, as well as the guard-tackle. The technique is the same for any two line-men who do it.

The center's block is the hardest block on this play. The center's rule is to block the first defensive linemen away from the call. Your center has to be better than the 1 or 2 technique he is blocking because this block is a bitch. He is going to ANGLE DRIVE the backside. We call it that because it is a drive block that has to be executed at an angle. People think it is easy. I've got four centers still playing in the NFL, and it was a bitch for all of them. The center has to step relative to the technique of the 2 technique. All I tell him is to get to the area where the landmark is supposed to be. The center has the reader, who cross face the center when they see his step. You have other guys that simply blow their butt upfield. The game plan will dictate the technique the center is going to use.

We keep our center in a two-point stance for this purpose. I feel he can step better that way. He steps with his onside foot and tries to get his head across the bow of the defender. What we try to do is step with our left foot, get the head across, and try to pin the hip of the 2 technique with his right hand. He probably can't pin that hip, but it gives him a surface to block so he can hold onto his butt, because that is what he is trying to do. We try to pin the hip and take him away from the call. If you don't have a good center, you can use the reverse block using the same target. On contact the center flips his hips into the hole. Defensive linemen don't like this type of block. This is the answer we give our guys when they are having trouble cutting off the 2 technique. That is the "down" part of the down and around blocking scheme.

Now let's talk about the "around" part of this play. Line coaches are the ultimate schemers. They are always trying to come up with ways to block. But you have to keep it simple for the guys who have to do the blocking. Your schemes are not worth anything if your meatheads can't perform it. We want to REVISIT CREATIVITY. How can we keep this play the same, but help them at the same time? It is all about finding the things that your guys do best. If it ain't simple, I don't want to do it. There is no such thing as a complicated play. If it's complicated, it ain't worth anything. The fun part of this play is the guard and tackle pull. The backside guard is going to pull and trap the 6 technique area. All we tell him is he is to go a hundred miles an hour. He is going to blow up the 6 technique area.

There are a lot of different ways to pull. Here is what we teach. We rip our elbow out, drop-step, and target. We don't want to get too deep. We target relative to the technique we have to block. A coaching point for the guard is not to get too tight to the center. If they do, when they rip their arm, they could hit the ball and cause a fumble. When we run these types of plays, we widen our splits a little. The extra width gives the blocker a momentary advantage to see what he has to find. He pulls, targets, sprints hard, and blows up the 6 technique area. We have to be lower than the defensive end and create horizontal movement. If the defensive end wrong-arms him, he plays football with a nasty attitude. He doesn't have time to key anything. If the end wrong-arms him, we still try to blow him up.

The tackle pulls for the first call-side linebacker. I tell him to pull and trap the call-side linebacker. I don't know where he is going to be and neither does that tackle. The tackle has to widen so he can get his spacing with the guard. If the guard does his job, the tackle has to be able to see the hole to get up on that linebacker. A tackle who gets too close to his guard can't get inside or outside. The only thing he can do is stack up the play. It is not the depth of the tackle, it is the width of his split. If the tackle reads the wrong arm technique by the defensive end on the guard, he goes outside and looks back inside for the linebacker. Nothing has changed for him.

The fullback, or motion man, or whoever it is, blocks the picket fence on the back side. They block the backside C Gap area. The tailback takes his steps to the back side, takes the ball, and runs downhill to cram the ball in the C Gap. He is running on the hip of the tackle. He is reading the tackle's block. We can run this play from Two Backs, One Back, or any amount of formations, and from motion. What we have done is created a whole offense from one scheme.

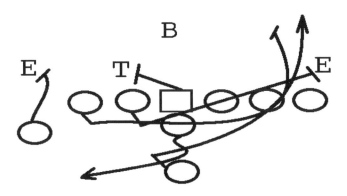

We can block this by pulling one guard. We take the fullback and replace the guard. The guard replaces the tackle. This is not a counter, but it is the same play for the linemen. The guard takes his split, pulls down the line, and tracks the call-side linebacker. The tackle now becomes the picket man to the back side. He steps inside and protects the B Gap. If nothing shows, he steps out on anything coming outside.

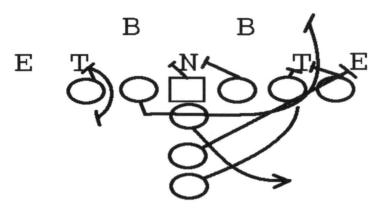

Those are two plays and two base ways to run to a tight end or an open-end side. The good thing is both of these plays are taught exactly the same way. They are not the same play but are in the same premise. If a team tries to stop these two plays, our first answer is Play Action Pass. You can't be hard headed and run the play when the defense is effectively stopping it. If you still want to run the play, adjust it.

If the guard is getting stoned by the wrong arm technique of the defensive end and the tackle can't catch the linebacker, we adjust the play. We can add a term; in our case we add SWEEP. The play becomes a Counter Sweep. The play looks the same. The guard gets a little depth in his pull. He logs the defensive end this time instead of trapping him. We want him to get depth so he can get outside leverage. We want him to cut the defensive end's outside leg. The tackle pulls. As he gets to the center he gets depth to about 3 yards. It is an automatic log by the guard, and he is going around the corner. The first two steps look exactly like the Counter Trap. The coaching point we tell the tailback is to get his shoulders toward the sideline. That is an answer when you are having trouble with the Counter Trap. We haven't changed a thing except our coaching points.

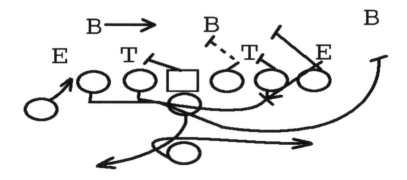

To run this play you have to drill it. To run this play the linemen have to react to what they see. You can start drilling this during the winter program. It teaches the short pull and long pull. We line up two lines of guys. You can go one at a time or two at a time. That's up to you. We want them to pull, react to what they see, and change direction. That is extremely important for an offensive lineman. If a lineman cannot redirect, I don't want him. The guard pulls and targets the cone. He sprints to the cone and turns up. As soon as he turns up, there is a coach right there that gives him a direction. He reacts to the coach and redirects in the direction the coach has pointed. What this teaches the tackle is this: As he comes up in the hole the line-backer is not going to be standing still, waiting for him. That line-backer is going to be on the move. The tackle has to find him, redirect his path to get to him, and then block him. We set one cone at 8 yards and one at 4 yards. That lets them practice the long and short pulls. We check their running form to make sure they are running over their pads. If they get too high they lose their leverage. Everything in offensive line blocking is leverage.

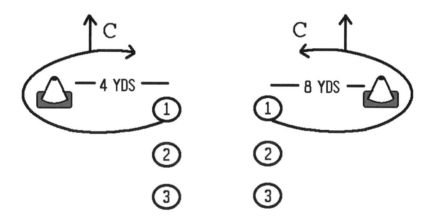

The next thing we do is put in a manager in the place of the coach. We put a towel behind his back tucked into his pants. We give the manager a little box drawn on the ground. The managers hate this drill because they get beat up. As the tackle comes around the cone, he has to go get the towel from the manager. The manager can run around in that box to avoid the lineman. It is a fun drill and it teaches the lineman to stick his foot in the ground as he rounds the cone. Once the lineman gets in the box he has to chase the towel until he gets it. We make the box small so that it is one move by the manager and then they get him.

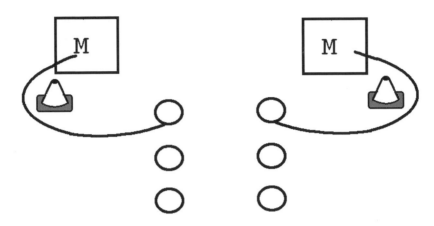

Don't do a drill just to do a drill. That is worthless. When I do a drill I want it to be completely applicable to what we do. In this drill we are using a slide pull technique like a sweep play. The guard has a one-on-one block with a linebacker. We are trying to teach eye read and angle to the block. The tackle is blocking down, and the guard is pulling for the linebacker. He keeps his shoulders parallel to the line of scrimmage as he pulls. We set up cones to represent the tackle and tight end gaps. They have to have their eyes on the linebacker, but they have to feel where the tackle and tight end gaps are. The coach stands behind the guard and signals the defender where to go. The defender has flags on like a flag football belt. The defender blows the hole where the guard pulled from, or runs through the tackle gap, or runs through the end gap, or just runs outside the end gap. The guard pulls and grabs the flag or towel or whatever you are using. We don't let the linemen touch the cones. They have to weave their way through the cones and grab the towel. We work them both ways, going two at a time.

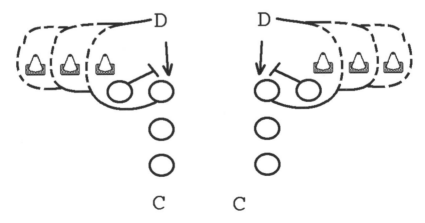

This next drill is for the guard and tackle working their pulls in the Counter Trap. We set up the spacing for the play. We have the right side pulling left and the left side pulling right. We have a dummy holder in the 6 technique area. I give them directions for what I want them to do. They go upfield with the bag, come down, or come down inside. The guard has to read the target and get his path relative. The tackle is reading the guard's path and reacting accordingly. It is a rapid-fire drill with four guys going at once. You can do the same drill with the fullback and the guard.

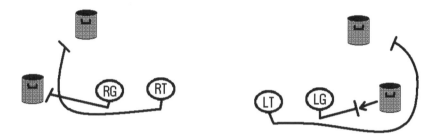

Those are three drills to work on pulls. The key coaching points, as I go through these drills are (1) chest on the knee, (2) head up and targeting, (3) bent knees, and (4) run through the block with great explosion. The only thing that gets me concerned is that they get to the block on time. I don't worry so much if their footwork is not exactly right. If they are hustling and giving good effort, I'm not too concerned about trivial things.

Chapter 9

TIGHT END BLOCKING TECHNIQUES

By
Greg Meyer
Northwestern University
1996

The first thing I want to share with you is my impression of what I thought a tight end was. When I started coaching at Arizona State, I felt the tight end was a pass receiver first and a blocker second. That was what I liked doing and what I liked to see happening. My experience had been with quarterbacks and tight ends. Then I had the chance to go with Coach Gary Barnett to Northwestern. When he gave me the chance to coordinate the offense, I became much more knowledgeable about the running game because of my experience with tight ends. I don't think we have all the answers, but our offensive line coach was very patient with me. There was a lot of teaching I had to get involved with between the tight ends and tackles. What I found out was that I became much more excited about the running game and about the blocking techniques than I ever knew existed at Arizona State.

I think as a coach, the greatest way to teach a young man what his responsibilities are is to have great communication. We give the athlete a word for every single technique that he has to utilize to execute his block. You will hear these terms. We not only identify the technique of the defender, but we identify the technique the tight end has to use to execute that block.

The other thing we use is called "muscle memory." For your players to make the correct steps into a block, they must take training through "muscle memory." The other part of the training is for them to do it without tipping the defense as to which way they are going. Stance and steps are things we do every day. We want our players to get into a stance so they can take the steps they need without taking false or cheat steps. Once they know the stance we want them in, they have to work to get the weight mentally transferred so they can take the correct step without the cheat or false steps.

This is critical. They have to be able to transfer the weight consciously. The next thing they have to do is transfer the weight subconsciously. They have to get the feel so that the move is natural where they can do it without thinking. When that tight end comes to the line of scrimmage, he has to look at the defensive front, listen for the line call, listen for any automatic the quarterback may make, and think about the block. The last thing you want in his head is what foot he is going to step with and how he is going to do it. We have guys that have been in our program for three years and still have a hard time stepping. Our tight ends get into left- and right-handed stances depending on the side they are lined up on. We do this so they are more effective executing the blocks. To get comfortable in a left-handed stance takes time away from practice. The ends must work on their own away from the practice field to get that natural feeling. We don't have time to work as long as it takes to get that attitude done. For some it comes natural, but if it doesn't, they have to put in the extra time.

Because the defense wants to put pressure on the passer, they widen the outside end and use a speed rush. The offensive line coach counters that move by putting the tight end to that side. That makes the tight end a pass blocker. His stance helps him in that respect.

The next thing I'll talk about is "power angles." Power angles are proven facts from physics. The first thing in the power angle is to work hard to keep your feet moving. Work on flexibility with your players. The better and more flexible your players are in their ankles, the better chance they have of having good power angles with a good solid base. Some guys have to get back on their heels to stay low in a good football position. That is the last thing you want. You want them on the balls of their feet, but you want the entire shoe on the ground. To do this, you have to bend your knees and have good flexibility in your ankles. We want the knees, feet, and back going straight down the field with the foot in total contact with the ground. We do this in a drill. We call it a "Duck Walk" or "Power Strut." All we want them to do is get their toes going forward and step in that position planting their foot every time for about 5 yards. If they are on the balls of their feet and meet resistance, they fall back on their heels. But if their feet are solid on the ground, they have a good solid base. If the knees move outside, that destroys the power of physics because the power is going in two different directions. An example of creating a good power angle and losing it is a common tendency for most blockers. If the tight end is on a front-side block or cutoff block, he gets inside-out leverage. That puts him in a good power position, but the first thing he wants to do is turn his hips into the hole. As soon as the tight end puts his hips in the hole or turns his shoulders, he has destroyed his power angles. All the good work we have done to get the power going in one direction is lost. Now the defender squeezes him right back into the hole.

The line of force includes the alignment of feet, hips, and shoulders parallel to our desired line of force. The forearm, head, and shoulders are our blocking surface. The hips and legs are the power source. The feet are the wheels. When the blocker strikes his initial blow at a point, he must be low enough and close enough, and he must continue to make the block work. He has to be low enough to create a lifting force on the defender. He has to be close enough to neutralize his charge. The force must be continued to get the defender on his heels so he is unable to make a counter move.

I am starting to believe that a bunched stance is better for our tight ends. It does not look good. It looks goofy. In the bunched stance we look like a frog in our stance. I don't care as long as we are able to execute and do the things a tight end has to do. The reason I like the bunched stance is better balance after the first step, it is good for power angles on contact, and it gives us better vision. We ask the tight end to alert blockers to secondary backs in blitz modes. They have to see coverages and secondary alignments. We can better do that from a bunched stance.

We feel, regardless of the technique, once the end knows what his assignment is, his step is going to take him directly to his aiming point. The only exception would be a defender playing heavy on the tight end. In that case we might false key with the head. We are going to step normally in the direction of our aiming point. The only difference will be the length of the step. The length of the step will depend on the type of block he's trying to execute. The defender is going to react as soon as the end moves. The longer the end has his foot off the ground, the less chance he has of getting a good base. We want them stepping with the correct foot in the right direction, but we want the foot picked up and put down as quickly as they can do it. We want to keep a good center of balance within the framework of their body when they block a base scheme. A base scheme to us is the inside and outside zone play. His rule is Man On or Man On Outside if we were running the outside zone play.

In the base scheme, the end aims one inch outside the sternum. The end picks up the outside foot and short steps. This gives the defender the impression we are trying to hook him. It is not a long step. It is a short influence step. We want the blocker to picture a rod running down the center of his body when he is in the stance. The weight is mentally transferred to the inside foot. If the defender is a head reader, the end can turn his head to add to the influence. When we execute the base block, we stretch the defender by the outside step and maybe the head turn. But the second step has to start pressuring back inside to get the inside out leverage. If he has physically transferred his weight to the outside, he has to physically transfer it back to the inside on the next step. If too much weight flows outside, the end has to bring it all back. We want the defender to flow outside and pressure him inside.

The next part of blocking is the "punch and hip roll." We used to teach on the first step to get the arms back and cocked for the punch. In the NFL our kids are telling us they are not looking for that big cocking motion any more. Even though offensive line coaches were stressing it, it is almost impossible to do. Most coaches can't tell whether contact is made on the first or second step. We tell our players to be ready to punch as quickly as they can. During the first step the hands have to come up into the cocked position. We don't want our players just getting their hands on the defender and pushing. We want to punch through the defender, not to him. If you are working on bags to teach the punch, don't let them stop on the second step and punch. Make them punch and go on to the third and fourth step. We call it punch and go. We want to use the entire surface of the feet when possible. That allows them to stay in balance and maintain a wide base for the power angles. We teach the bunched stance, but once they come out of the stance their base widens.

The "CUTOFF SCHEME" is the next thing I want to cover. In this scheme we step with the foot that we are cutting off with. The distance and angle of the cutoff block is determined by the alignment of the defense. The first step has to make up distance without overextending the base. If the end has to cut off a man who is over our tackle, he knows he can't take a big enough step without overextending the base. The further inside the cutoff, the flatter the inside step must be. If the end is cutting off a 9 technique, he wouldn't take a flat step. He takes an angle step unless the defender is doing an awful lot of veering inside. The aiming point is to get the opposite cheek on the inside hip of the defender. If the cutoff can't be made, the end continues to push the defender with his shoulders square across the hole so when the cutback comes, it goes outside of him.

In the second step, our goal is to create inside-out leverage without losing our base. He maintains his power angles and keeps his shoulders square. He wants to avoid turning his hips and shoulder too soon.

A lot of coaches tell their players they have to be mean and aggressive all the time. We use a "Butt Block." This occurs when the end has gone for the inside hip and feels the defender coming off his backside. It has the appearance of an overreached cutoff block. All we want from our end is to screen the defender from the play. He uses his butt to screen him off the play. We don't want him to try to turn around and block him. If he does that, the defender will be around him and have a chance to make the play. We don't tell our people to work for the butt block, but we don't discourage them from using it. If you tell your ends they have to be physical and not use the butt block, they will start to hesitate and get beat across their faces.

We fight pressure with pressure. Some of the biggest plays in the zone play come off the backside cutoff block. Once the end gets his cheek to the inside hip, he fights pressure to the outside. He doesn't try to turn his hips, but keeps his shoulders square and works outside. If the defender gets across his head, he still fights the pressure, but takes him down inside.

In the cutoff block, maintaining contact for as long as possible is critical. Just getting to the cutoff position is not enough. The end has to stay on his block and continue to keep his feet moving because the play has a chance of cutting back to his block. The last thing that could happen is for the end to have stepped inside and the defender is rushing outside. If that occurs, the end pushes him on by the hole. That makes the end's job easy, because he has run himself out of the play.

To communicate to the tight end the defensive alignment of the defender, we use numbers. We call a defender aligned head up on the tight end a 6 technique. Defenders on the inside shade or eye of the tight end are in a 7 technique. A defender on the outside shoulder or eye of the tight end is in a 9 technique.

Our offensive plays are called even-numbered plays toward the tight end and odd-numbered plays away from him. The tight end moves from side to side according to the formation, and with him comes the even-numbered plays. I'm not saying that is good or bad. In our system it works. Our tight end knows if he hears "38" or "32" it is a play-side run. That is regardless of whether he is on the left or right side of the formation. The tackle knows the same thing. If there is an odd call, they know they are in some kind of cutoff mode. When we run the inside zone play, if the tight end is covered, his assignment is "Base." The term "Base" is also a technique. If we are running the outside zone play, "38," and the end and tackle are covered, his assignment is "Mo." The term "Mo" is his technique. "Mo" stands for "Man on Outside." The end takes a six-inch step to stretch the defender. The back can either cut up or go outside.

On the inside zone play, "32" with the tackle uncovered and the end with a 7, 6, or 9 technique on him, the rule is "Ace." That is an uncovered rule for us. "Ace" tells the tackle and end they are in a combination scheme from down linemen to the linebacker. The ball is going inside. If the tackle is uncovered and the ball is going outside, the rule, scheme, and technique is called "Uno." That puts the tackle and tight end on a combination block down linemen to the linebacker.

When the ball goes away from the tight end, the tight end has some kind of cutoff scheme. We name the cutoff so the tight end knows what type of technique he has to use. In our normal inside zone play our scheme is a "Wall" or "Base Cutoff" depending on if the tackle is covered or uncovered. The "Wall" is used when the tackle and tight end are both covered. They simply wall the defender to the outside. Their blocks are extremely important because the ball could come back on a cutback. The "Base Cutoff" is used when the tackle is uncovered. With the "Wall" the tight end takes an outside step to set up the cutoff. On the "Base Cutoff" the tight end takes an inside step to the cutoff. By using the terms Wall and Base Cutoff, I know the tight end has recognized the front and knows what type of technique to use.

Teams will try to stunt off the back side to stop the inside zone play. If we are playing a stunting team we have to make an adjustment. The tight end and the tackle have a combination scheme called "Power Ed." If the defensive tackle and Sam linebacker are running crossing stunts, this call handles that. The tight end comes hard to the inside. If the Sam linebacker veers inside, the tight end is on him. The tackle reads his man going away and combines with the tight end on the Sam linebacker. If the defense runs the stunt the opposite way, which is more effective, the tight end comes hard inside and takes the looping tackle coming outside. The tackle reads his man going away and takes the Sam linebacker as he comes into the hole.

POWER ED vs SAM 1st

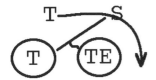

POWER ED vs SAM

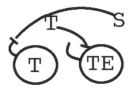

When we run the outside zone play away from the tight end, we use a "Scramble Cutoff" and a "Reach." The "Scramble Cutoff" is used when the end has to cut off a 7 technique defender. The ball is not going to cut back. All the end wants to do is keep the defender out of the pursuit lanes. The "Reach" is used to come down on a 5 technique with the ball going away.

Let me go back and talk about the "Ace" block. This is the tackle and tight end working in combination on a down lineman and a linebacker. The first thing we tell our tight end and tackle is "feel the down man, and see the linebacker." We do that more so on the outside zone than the inside zone. Most of the time in the inside zone play the tackle ends up on the linebacker. The only time that wouldn't happen is if the down man veered to the inside. The tackle would end up on the down man, and the tight end would pick up the linebacker scraping over the top. The linebacker is seeing the same thing from the back on the inside or outside zone play.

For the linebacker to be effective on the outside zone play, he has to go in a hurry. If the linebacker is going to be a penetrator on this stunt he has to go hard with the flow. That makes him an easy target for the tight end. The tight end against a 6 or 9 technique steps with his outside foot to try to influence the defender. The tackle takes his feel step toward the tight end looking for the inside veer stunt. If there is a 7 technique on the tight end, he steps off with his inside foot. There will be no influence on the 7 technique defender. The tackle comes off to take away the inside veer by the 7 technique. He feels the down man and sees the linebacker. As long as the linebacker keeps his depth, the tackle will continue to help the tight end on the down man. The tight end knows he has the down man by himself when the tackle goes up on the linebacker.

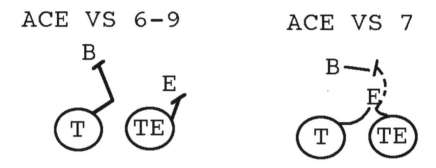

Here are the main points in the inside zone play. With the tackle and end covered, they block the base blocking scheme. The tight end steps with his outside foot to his aiming point, which is one inch outside the defender's sternum. He keeps his steps short and quick and tries to stretch the technique. He wants to keep his power angle in mind and center of gravity a little inside. He must be ready to work back inside after the first step. The idea is to stretch and then maintain inside-out leverage.

With the tackle uncovered and a 9, 6, or 7 technique on the tight end, we use the combination block. The tight end and tackle secure the down man first to the linebacker. Against a 9 technique, the end will turn into a base block. The first step of the tight end is determined by the technique of the defender. Any stunts between the linebacker and down lineman must be handled by the tight end and tackle. Always maintain inside-out leverage, fight pressure, and continue to stress power angle principles.

On the outside zone play where the tackle and tight end are covered, we use a "MO" block scheme. The tight end takes a six-inch lateral step to the outside hip of the defender. The wider the technique, the wider the angle of departure, but don't overstep. The tight end keeps his power angle in mind and his center of gravity as close to the center as possible. If he gets the inside veer by the defender, he has to handle that. The tight end continues to stretch the defender until the defender's momentum takes him too wide, then he turns out and runs the defender to the sideline.

If the tackle is uncovered, he works his Uno combo block with the tackle. He works with the tackle to block the down lineman to the frontside linebacker. The tackle has to feel the down man and see the linebacker. The tight end's first step depends on the alignment of the defender. If the defender is head up, the tight end steps with his outside foot. He takes a 6-inch power step to make contact on the first step if possible. He tries to keep his shoulders as square as possible. The tackle wants to cover the linebacker up. It is not always necessary or best to wall the linebacker off. If the tight end or tackle covers up the linebacker, the back will make his cut. If the tight end has a 9 technique on him, the blocking scheme becomes the MO scheme. If the defender is in a 7 technique and veers, the tight end cannot leave his tackle out on an island. Penetration kills this play. If the veer stunt comes too quickly for the tackle, the tight end has to punch hard to slow down the defender and give the tackle a chance to get on him. He does not turn and chase him down inside. He has to punch, keep his shoulders square, and run the linebacker outside if he has to.

Chapter 10

FUNDAMENTALS OF LINE BLOCKING

By
Joe Moore
University of Notre Dame
1994

Anytime I have been around a coach, I always wanted to know what he is thinking and what he is teaching. First of all, if you are going to be a Line Coach you must believe that your tackle can block their defensive tackle, or that your guard can block their guard or linebacker. You must believe that your players can block someone. If you think you must have a scheme to move the ball, then you have a serious problem because no matter how much you work with a player he will know if you do not believe in him. They know what you believe. You must actually believe in what you are teaching. You have to believe you can block a man.

It is a proven fact if a team can't run the football, then you can't win unless you have a great defense. I have been around a lot of passing game experts, and I have been at schools where passing game experts have come in. Anytime we have adopted the passing game we have had to depend on our defense to win football games. If you can't run the football, and you do not believe your men can block the men up front, you have to depend on your defense. I am not trying to tell you that you do not have to have a scheme, but if you think you can throw the ball and win, you are better than I am.

There is one thing I have found since I have been in college coaching. When we find players from high school that have been taught to block when they get to us in college, that high school coach has a winning record. Almost always. I can't think of any lineman that we have gotten that was ready to play where the high school coach was not a winning coach. There must be some correlation between offensive line play and winning. We see a lot of big linemen. I must have turned down 30 players that were 6'6" to 6'7" that weighed 270 to 280 pounds. They could not block a pea off a pea pod. We took some kids that were 6'3" and 6'4" from those schools that were winning and playing for championships that were better blockers. It has been that way ever since I have been in college coaching. Teams that know how to run the ball and know how to block win. You have to teach them how to play the positions and you must get the athletes.

It is important to talk to the best people in football. I never took a job where I could not take one of my assistants with me and go visit for one week in the off-season. If I take a job, I want one week where I can go observe football. I never asked for anything else. I never asked how much money I was making; but I made sure I got one week to go visit other schools. I always want a chance to improve myself. Right now at Notre Dame I plan to go visit other schools. It is so important. You do not need to just sit and listen, you need to go watch people coach. I never talked to a line coach in my life that was not just knocking the crap out of people. Watch them coach, I do not care who they are.

I used to drive by a school that was always working on a Seven-Man Sled. I figured we had a chance to beat that team. I went to visit with them one day and asked the coach why he used the sled so much. He told me the sled helped them get off the ball at the same time. I am not too smart, but I do know this. If they all got off the ball at the same time, they are not getting off as the fastest man, but they are getting off together with the slowest man. If you can watch seven men at the same time you are better than I am. I have trouble watching a man's left arm. I have trouble watching seven at one time. If you can watch seven men at one time you should be on *Saturday Night Live*. I am not against the Seven-Man Sled for conditioning. If you want to condition kids after practice you can. If you start coaching them when they are working on conditioning you are wasting your time.

I do not believe in using the Boards to teach blocking. I have talked to coaches that said they used boards to teach the players to keep their feet apart. If you can't teach them to keep their feet apart without using boards, you need to look at what you are doing. When I have seen coaches using boards I see two things; the head is down and the ass is up in the air.

One thing I do believe in is Strength. The number 1 area where you need strength is in the legs. Kids like to work with the arms because it makes them look better in T-shirts.

I talk to a lot of good football coaches about strength in the legs. They all stress the Squat for the legs. If you get nothing else out of this get the kids doing the Squat to build their leg strength. You can't play football unless you can bend in the knees and hips. Squats are very important. These are things I have always wanted to know when I talked to other coaches. I never once asked another coach for a play. I never asked anyone how he ran a play. If you ever watched us on offense you would know that, because my offense never was that good. We played good defense and ran the ball off tackle. One reason I never wanted to get a play from another coach was because I did not want to end up calling him to ask him what we should do when the defense did something different. I have always been sold on fundamentals and defense. Once in a while we could get the ball in the end zone. I think you can win with one play if everyone plays his position as opposed to 100 plays and no one knows what they are doing. I am a basic fundamental coach. I like pure and simple. At Notre Dame, Coach Holtz likes to run a lot of different plays. I have been there six years now. Slowly, Coach Holtz is coming over to my way because I can't learn his way. We are limited on what we do on offense. You win on fundamentals.

The first thing you have to learn to do is to learn how to be a coach. If I see someone teaching something that I think is wrong, or if I think he is teaching it wrong, it makes me a better coach. Always challenge your mind and your thoughts. Always try to get better. Always associate with winners. Now, we are always going to have champions. Someone is going to win the Super Bowl next year, the Big Ten, the SEC, the Rose Bowl, and all other championships. That does not mean they are good coaches. Someone has to win the championship. If a team is winning consistently, I will guarantee you are going to find consistent play in fundamentals.

I want to list the things I teach in fundamentals. The number one thing is STANCE. People ask what is Stance? The number 1 thing when you put them in a stance is this: They must be able to move in any direction that the offense requires without any false movement. It is that simple. If they have to take a false step or a false movement, then you need to change the stance. I have had some kids that never became fluid in their stance. If they are a good athlete, it is impossible for them not to have a stance where they can accomplish what you ask them to do. You must take the time to teach them. Stance is this. A man has to perform whatever you ask him to do without making any false movement. If a player does not have a good stance, he is going to struggle as a football player. The only way you will know if they have a good stance is by studying the film. Look for false movement. We all have VCR's. You can get films of practice if you really want them. Don't just take team films. Take individual shots of the linemen. Look at their stance. See if they are making any false moves.

A basic rule would be that your feet can never be too wide in your stance. We know you could be too wide, but most of the time in the stance the feet are too close together. So we start with this premise; most people have their feet too close together on the stance. We like for the toes to be turned out and the heels turned inside slightly. I know a lot of teams like to teach the heels out and the toes pointed inside. If you are teaching that, it is fine. I have looked at film after film and I can't find anyone who plays with the toes turned inside.

We stagger the feet on the stance. It all depends on what you want to teach. If it hinders his movement, then it is wrong. I like the hand directly down under the chin. The more you put your hand out in front of you, the more off balance you are. It makes it hard to block down, and hard to pull, and hard to pass block. You can almost play without the hand on the ground. It all comes back to this one thing. Can he do all the things he needs to do without any false movement. I like the hand down on the ground under his chin. This is true even with the center. They want to call us offside because the center has his hand past the ball.

The first step is to get you into position to make a block. If a man is playing head up and you are going to base block him you do not have to worry much because the first step is right there. If the man is in the position you want him in, the first step is there. The first step is almost always with the near foot. Our rule is to step with the near foot first. Very seldom do we have to correct a kid on this. If the blocker has to block with someone on the back side then we may use the far foot. We do not step with the back foot unless we are using the combo block.

The next most important point is to have an aiming point. The near foot leads to that aiming point. Now, I favor the three-point stance. I would rather have a two-point stance than a four-point stance. So, we want to get in a good stance and then find the aiming point. After that we must get Pad under Pad. It is a "LEVERAGE GAME." If the two players are equal, the man with leverage will win every time. If you are not equal, the leverage man will win most of the time. If the blocker stinks, and the defensive man is great, leverage will not matter.

The sole purpose of the block is to get to the man's chest. His whole purpose is to keep the blocker away from his body. Try to get to his chest. I do not believe in blocking with the face mask. I never have. You must get the shoulder pad under his pad. If you can get to his chest and get your pad under his pad, you have a great chance to block him. The elbows must be kept inside. I try to coach the lineman from two different positions. I try never to get to the side of the blockers. I like to coach from behind or from the front. The main thing I look for are the elbows. If I can see the elbows from behind he is not blocking properly. I do not teach him a lot of things with the hands. I teach him to get on the man with the pads, and keep the feet moving, and to keep the elbows in. If you start stressing the hands too much, you lose the other key points. We do teach them to use their hands, but we stress the other things much more. We feel the hands will take care of themselves. Don't get me wrong, the hands are important. I am not saying that our kids don't hold. We do not teach them to hold and tackle on offense.

The blocker must lead with his eyes and not his face mask. He must lead with his eyes. That is when the coach must get in front of the blocker to make sure he is leading with his eyes. You are better off coaching from the front than any other position. He must look his block in.

I do not believe in any windup. Your feet must be under the blocker. We want to keep the knees up under us. I never mention the word feet except to tell them to get them wide on their stance. Their legs must go with the blocker. That is where the strength is. If the feet are not up under the blocker, the first thing that happens is he loses contact. He must get on and stay on the defender. The blocker must be able to bend naturally. If you can't bend, you can't be a football player.

When I am talking to coaches that have not studied films I know that person does not know what he is talking about. I have talked to coaches that have been in the game 30 to 40 years. They have watched films, but they have never studied the films. I know they do not study the films when they tell me they roll the hips. We do not roll the hips. People will roll the hips but they will do it naturally. You cannot teach something that happens naturally. We want movement. We start down low and come up. If we roll our hips as we come up we lose our strength.

We want to keep the helmet to the play side. We will have one-on-one drills to teach all of these points. We have drills where they must keep their helmet to the play side. This is where the elbows and hands come into play. The strength is inside with the arms and hands. We do not want them to turn the defender. We want to get movement on the defender. If we get leverage on them we want to take them straight back. We do not want the defender to cross the helmet to the play side. If the blocker has his feet up under him and the elbows are in, it is more difficult for the defender to cross the helmet. When the feet stop, you lose your leverage. We like to film as much as we can so the kids can watch and learn what they are doing on their blocks. One other thing I have learned about coaching. Defensive coaches are nice people, but you can't trust them. They will lie to you. They will lie, cheat, and do everything to look good in practice. So, I do not even bother with them. I never ask our defensive coaches what they are doing. I have no idea what front they are running in practice and I don't care. All I know is this: Anytime they ever told me they were using a front it was the one they were using yesterday. Don't get involved with all of that crap. You can get a defensive coach who will allow you to base block against and do the fundamentals against.

Let me review real fast. First is stance. The kids are going to do what you tell them to do without any false steps. Teach them the importance of leverage. We want movement and we want to keep our body under us. If they feel the man is disengaging we want them to accelerate. We want movement. We want them to bust their rear ends to stay after the man when we feel them getting off the block.

I want to show you our run blocking. I want you to see our Trap blocking. Everyone knows we are going to run the Trap but we still average close to 7 yards on it. Let me cover the running part real quick. Anytime we do a run drill we go 10 yards. We want them to run through the 10 yards on any drill we use. We trap the 3 technique so much we limit what he is going to do.

I am not big on X's and O's. I really don't like X's and O's. I am not saying you do not have to have them. I know you can't win without them. We came up with something that we feel is good and we are willing to share what we do.

Does anyone want to know what we do down on the Goal Line? When we get down deep we want to get at least three points. We like to run the bootleg on the Goal Line. I know the blocking schemes, but I do not get involved in the pass patterns. When they start talking about pass patterns I leave the room.

If you are good enough to run the ball and you get real good at it, this is what you are going to see. We are going to see the Eight-Man Front with a Safety playing on the Tight End. They have a Corner on each side playing Man-to-Man. That is basically what we see when we start moving the ball on the run. We see this on first down all of the time. We have more than 150 pass patterns. When we get moving the ball on the run and people know they can't stop us, they will go to a Nine-Man Front with the Strong Safety playing the run. They are not playing Man Free, they are Man-to-Man on the Corners. They lock on the receivers with the Free Safety running. Now, how much imagination does it take to take a man out of the backfield to get him open? They have been drawing up pass patterns for 150 years. Do you know why? Because they can't run the football. They have a coverage for every pass pattern.

I could be a Defensive Coordinator because all you have to do is assign someone to play Man-to-Man on the pass receivers. That is all you have to do. If you will show me a Passing Coach, I will show you that they will not win unless they play great defense. If you want to win you run the ball. Teach discipline and run the ball and you will win. Run the ball effectively and you will get Single-Man Coverage.

This is another thing that gets me about passing the football. The offensive linemen are told to defeat the defender in front of them in a small area about four feet by four feet. The receivers can split outside and now they have 10 yards to beat the man covering him. Now, you tell me about passing the football. All of you are passing coaches. Run the ball first and then it is easy to pass.

Another thing we like to do on the Passing Game is to use Motion. We like to take those little guys and bring them in Motion and then run the patterns. That is effective against Man Coverage.

I want to talk about the Zone Play. If you are going to run the Zone Play you should use Motion. This gives the defense a different look. If you can run the ball you will get Man Coverage. The receivers should be able to get open against one defender. I am not a passing man, but I do believe in the Passing Game. You cannot win unless you can throw the football. If you can run the football the defense can only run certain things against you. If you cannot run the football you will see every defense that has ever been designed by man. They are drawing some of them up now. If you can run the football, the defense is limited down to almost nothing. What most teams have started doing is this. They will go to the Nine-Man Fronts and

Play Man. "They ain't going to beat us with the run. If they beat us they must do it with the Passing Game." If you can make them say this, then you throw the ball. If you can't throw the ball, you are wasting your time. You must be able to throw the football to go against all of those men up on the line of scrimmage. Run the ball; the rest comes easy.

Chapter 11

OFFENSIVE LINE TECHNIQUES

By
Don Riley
University of Kentucky
1993

If I gave my talk a topic it would be Transferring the Oklahoma Drill to Run to Daylight. It is important for us to remember what we are attempting to do when we set up our drills. We do not want to set the dummies up so they are only 1 yard apart on the Oklahoma Drill the first time we teach the drill. We want to show the players what we are trying to accomplish. We want to open up the holes so the back can run to daylight. Move the dummies 2 yards apart so we can give the offensive linemen an advantage to start out with. I think you have to be honest with the players you deal with. Trust is the most important ingredient for success. They trust you, and you trust them. This is the way I approach the players I work with.

I tell the players that I know that somewhere along the way they had other ideas about being a linebacker, fullback, or some other football player other than an offensive lineman. Somewhere along the way someone told them they were not good enough to play another position so they moved them to the offensive line. I tell them this. "If you were as good as the player you are blocking, I would not be coaching you. We want you to understand our view. We want to give you all the tools that we can that will allow you to be successful." We tell them we are not going to put them into a situation where they can not be successful. We are going to put them in a position where they can be a winner.

We all have been to clinics and listened to talks on stance. It all comes down to what you believe in as a coach. I am convinced after several years of coaching that we had to widen our stance because of pass protection. We used to say get the feet as wide as the armpits. Now we say get the feet as wide as the shoulders' width. If you have a narrow base, you can be turned easier. We want to make sure we start with a slightly wider stance.

The next thing we want to tell our young people is this: You block with your hips. You must learn how to use your hips. Next we tell them to drive with the eyes. They have to focus with their eyes. I can remember going to hear Blanton Collier lecture when I first started coaching. He made things so simple. He talked about how important the eyes were in playing football. He stressed where their eyes go on everything they do in football.

Sometimes we overemphasize hip extension. We throw our hips, and at times we throw the hips down. When they go down so far, it causes us to arch our backs. All the defender has to do is to get his hands under us and lift us up to get rid of us. When you drive off you have to drive your knees down. When you start lifting you bring your knees up because your hips are following through. You want to explode your hands and forearms up under the defender's pads.

I do not know how many of you ever saw a Mule-Pulling Contest. Being from the coal mining country, I saw the mules pulling coal out of the mines. When a mule is in a pulling contest they hook up big sleds for the mules to pull. They really bend their knees and work with their backs. They keep their feet close to the ground. They do this so they can have power and balance. They keep their feet really wide. This is the way it is with the offensive linemen. On contact he must widen his feet. If the feet are wide when the defensive blow is made, you have a chance to keep your balance. One of the real key ingredients for an offensive lineman is to have balance. You can't have balance with a narrow base. Now, you want your feet wide, drive off, and lock up. What happens a lot of the time is the blocker tries to finish the job before it is necessary. You must learn that the defender that you are blocking has been told by his coach to make the tackle. What you have to do is to lock up with the defender with your feet wide. You have to use powerful steps with the knees down. Once you feel the defender trying to disengage and get off the block, you must react. To get off the block the defender is trying to get his hands away from you. That is the time you must accelerate your feet and then bring them together. That is the time you lift, climb him, and climb him. If you are climbing the defender and the back is running hard, his momentum will carry him forward and you will gain positive yardage. Those are selling points and are very important to use when he is teaching offensive blocking to his players.

The next point that is important for the offensive linemen to know is this: After studying the game of football for 30-plus years, it seems to me that if I had kept stats, more offensive linemen make tackles than defensive linemen. How many times have you seen offensive linemen making a block where they do not get their butts out of the hole and the back runs into the block. You have to get your butt out of the hole as a blocker. I think this next point is true for a blocker or tackler, regardless of the position you play. You must always block and/or tackle with the opposite hip. If you are blocking with the right shoulder you must accelerate the left hip to get your feet to move in front of the man. That is a very important point a player must learn to be a good lineman.

We believe this. For you to be a good offensive football team, you must give the game to your quarterback. You must find a way to make it simple so you can gain an advantage on the defensive structures that you are going to be facing each game. What we are saying is something like this. If you are going to run the football, we do not want to give the lineman an uphill block. We want to give him a downhill block. This is what I tell my players: If the funnel is wider, more water can go through it. If the funnel is small, less water can go through it. There are certain defenses that align themselves where we call plays and just hope they work. When we call a Pass Play, we call a protection and hope it works. They have to understand how defenses play. The most important thing an offensive coach can learn is not offense, but defense. HOW DO THEY PLAY? They are trying to stop you. As Patton said to Rommel, "I am going to read your book so I will know what you are trying to do to me." This is very important.

HOW DOES THE DEFENSE PLAY? We need a system for communication to discuss how they play. They are going to align somewhere. Now, I know everyone has his own system to communicate with the players. I was able to coach on the West Coast for 12 years. That was a great experience. I went to visit the four pro teams in the area and learned a great deal. I found there was something different about all four of them. That was good. I know that there is not ONE WAY to do a lot of things in football. It comes down to this. It is what you can teach your players that really counts. I will go over our techniques that we use at the University of Kentucky.

OFFENSIVE TECHNIQUES

Techniques — Defensive lineman alignment in relationship to the offensive lineman. The middle of the center is our 0 technique. Head up are Even techniques. The Gaps are Odd techniques. If the defender is on the outside of where the play is going we say he is in a Shade technique. If he is on the back side of the center we call that an "I" technique.

1. HEAD UP — EVEN NUMBERS

2. GAPS — ODD NUMBERS

3. OUTSIDE — "SHADE"

4. INSIDE — "I"

Our players will call out the techniques. They call out "Shade" or "I." These things mean something. This means there are certain things that we must understand in Gap Control as to whom we anticipate to be covering a certain area. Our blocking designs are set to block the defensive structures. If the linemen are lined up in the gaps between the center — guard, guard — tackle, and tackle — end gap, we say they are in the 1, 3, and 5 Gap. That may be contrary to what many of you are teaching today. If someone is threatening us, we can refer to the A, B, C, and D Gaps.

The quarterback can read the defense and tell the type of defense they are playing. We want to build a package to attack the defense. The number 1 package in America was what was started by Bud Wilkinson many years ago. It is a three-man front with four linebackers — the Oklahoma 5-4 Defense. We all know what that is. At the university we call this look the LSU Defense. We play LSU and they play this defense. All of my life I have been calling it the Oklahoma Defense. I am at Kentucky now and I have to call it what they call it. That is one of the standard defensive fronts that we know exist in football. We have three down linemen and four linebackers.

The other standard defensive front that we know about is with four down linemen and three linebackers. That is the standard 4-3 Defense. From these two fronts can come a multitude of alignments. I want to share some of the common fronts with you. Let me show you how it works. This is what I call America's Seven-Man Fronts. We take the LSU defense and take the tackle and move him down on the strong guard. That is what we call a Strong Eagle Defense. On the other side, if they take the weakside tackle and move him down on the guard, we call it a Weak Eagle. If they move the nose guard to the weak side we call it a Slide Weak. If the nose guard moves to the strong side we call it Slide Strong. We teach them compensation. When one man moves, then another man must move with him. When the linemen move in one direction, the secondary will move in the other direction. That is the way defenses work. They can anticipate the pass rush so they can get the right blocking angle on the defender.

We call a Stack Defense the Auburn Stack because they run this look. They can have a three-man front or a four-man front. We see a Stack 'Bama defense. They run their stack a little different. We see a Stack Diamond and a Double Eagle. We see a College 4-3 and a Pro 4-3 defense. That is all of the defenses we see. That is all we can see in terms of Gap Control.

AMERICA'S 7-MAN FRONTS

STRONG EAGLE

WEAK EAGLE

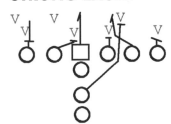

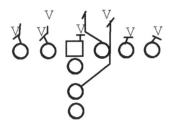

SLIDE WEAK

SLIDE STRONG

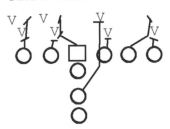

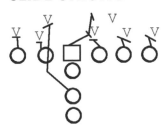

STACK AUBURN

STACK 'BAMA

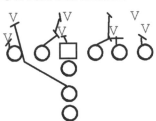

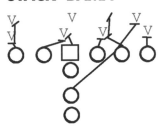

AMERICA'S 7-MAN FRONTS

STACK DIAMOND

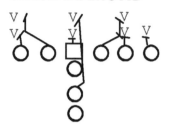

DOUBLE EAGLE

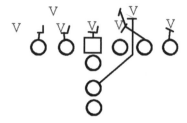

COLLEGE 4-3

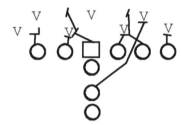

PRO 4-3

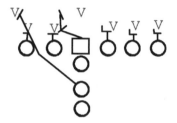

We want to understand the defense so we can plan our attack to Run to Daylight. Those who know Kentucky football know that we ran a new offense last year. I was fortunate to have coached at UCLA where we had some good tailbacks. We gave them the ball and let them Run to Daylight. We tried to isolate the defense and give them a base block and then let them run where fewer people were. Our plan at Kentucky is to have a plan from our Stack I alignment to run what we call the Blast Play. You can call it the Isolation or Blast Play. The Blocking Design is Lead Blocking. The Play Concept is a Daylight Play.

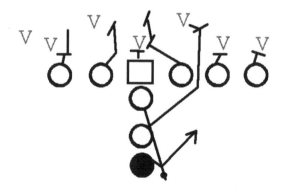

The tailback runs off the block of the first down lineman on the play side. It is run off the first down lineman the quarterback designates. The play can be run to the split end or the tight end. We allow our tailback to aim at the hip of the tackle. He can run the 500-pound bear; he can run where he wants to run. Our job is to stay off the ground and lock up on the blockers. When the defender tries to get off the block we want to accelerate our feet and get our butt out of the hole.

What are the BIG MUSTS on the play? We list the things that we must do on the play. You can block it two ways. You can block it Hard or Soft. This is the Hard blocking design.

BIG MUSTS

A. Hard ball play.

B. Inside leg of tackle landmark.

C. Ball carrier runs through daylight.

D. Blockers provide daylight.

E. Must have play-action pass that simulates onside blocking design.

It is important that you understand the concept and not the plays. You want to develop your offensive attack so the defenders see a picture that sometimes is false. He does not know whether to come up or go back. What happens on the sideline? The coach wants to know why he was dropping back instead of coming up. He yells, "I thought it was a pass." He becomes disoriented. It is important to have play-action passes with your running game.

Let me go over the blocking assignments on this Isolation Play. We do not write a lot of things up. We say we block defenses. We have a theory behind blocking defenses. We block defenses or techniques. Our quarterback will call out who has the base block. If the tackle is in a 4 technique the quarterback calls "Ringo 4." These are ideas, and are not specific. He might call "Ringo 2," "Ringo 6," "Lucky 4," or "Lucky 2." He is telling the man who has the base block. The general rule we give our line is this: If you are the first blocker inside the base block, you are to block away from the play. If we call RINGO RIGHT − 4, then the right guard will block down inside on the nose man. He will seal the defense. We are trying to run to daylight with a wider hole, seal the defense, put our fullback on the linebacker. We do not want to go right at the linebacker. We want it to look like a pass. He wants to run at the inside hip of the base block. The tailback is 7 yards deep and he knows where the base block will be. He is in no hurry. He will run to daylight.

ASSIGNMENTS

POSITION — ASSIGNMENT — CALLS

OSWR —

BSY - Base Block

OST - Base or Seal

OSG - Base or Seal

C - Base, Seal, or Scoop - Game Plan

BSG - Seal or Scoop

BST - Seal

BSWR -

FB - Block first linebacker being aware of Technique Call.

TB - Run off block on the first play-side defensive lineman. (Technique Call)

QB - Deep exchange - fake pass action. Ringo, Lucky, Opposite, Number.

One thing we are always working on is blocking schemes. We have certain calls. We always ask ourselves this question. HOW DO YOU BLOCK AN EAGLE DEFENSE? People on one side of the line cannot see the Eagle Look. We make sure our tackle calls out the Eagle defense so we all know the defense they are in on his side. We Slip block against the Eagle. We use the offside guard and center to wall off the defense. A Pro call means we face a middle linebacker. We have a call that we use called Away. This means we are going to seal away from the play. If the call is Ringo 4, and I am the right guard and I am uncovered, I am going to Slip block away from the play.

I have been hearing this statement since I was a little boy. "Knock him off the ball!" If you can do that you are going to win the ballgame. "Put him on his back!" Do you know when you put the defender on his back? When he is reaching to make the tackle and you accelerate your feet. That is when you can knock him on his back. What they are trying to say is this: COME OFF THE BALL.

The College 4-3 is a defense that you need to take a long look at. In theory, most teams who play a pro middle linebacker do not give him two gaps to defend, one on each side of the center. They will not give him A and A Gap; they give him A and B Gap on the same side of the line. Most of the time if you have the tight end in the game, they will have a man in the 2 Shade on that side. If you start running the Sweep Play, and cut the middle linebacker off with the Slip Block, they will find a way to move them outside. In most cases he will be in a 2 shade. If this is true then you can say that the middle linebacker rarely ever has both A Gaps. He may have the A Gap on one side on the flow, and the B Gap on the other side on flow. It is important that we understand this structurally.

When you are blocking with young people it is important for them to believe that the technique you are teaching is going to allow them to execute during the game. I went to UCLA in 1976 after 20 years of coaching. Terry Donahue was in his first year at UCLA. He was only 32 years old. Like all coaches, he wanted us to gain more wisdom to make us better coaches. Terry brought in people to help us learn more about people. He brought in a professor from the Physical Education Department to talk with us. Basically, what he told us was this: Do you know what running ropes will do for you? It will make you a good rope runner! Let's transfer that to our situation here: Do you know what the Oklahoma Drill will do for you? It makes you a better blocking team.

The thing about it is this. You must have an aptitude to make use of the Oklahoma Drill in your offensive system. If you can do that, the players will gain confidence in themselves because it will give them more success. They need all the success you can give them. You have to let them become successful. Make sure the drills you put your players in are applicable to the real game. If you can do that, I think it will improve your football game.

It is important to learn the fundamentals of the game. By learning this it will allow your people a chance to have success. Don't forget this important point. The man under the center is the man that can make a difference in widening the hole in the Oklahoma Drill. If he can make the calls for the offensive line, they will open the holes. Our rules for the quarterback to learn to call the defenses are not hard. We teach it in a systematic way and help him understand the All-American Defenses.

I want to close with this one aspect of coaching. Players want to know where they stand with you as a coach. I had a friend who did a study on what it takes to be a college lineman. He came up with this chart to measure the offensive lineman.

OFFENSIVE LINEMEN EVALUATION
NAME_____

RANKING	BENCH PRESS
Superior	100% - 420 - UP
Excellent	90% - 415 - 400
Very Good	80% - 395 - 375
Good	70% - 370 - 350
Average	60% - 345 - 320
Marginal	50% - 325 - 280

RANKING .... **POWER CLEAN**

Superior	100% - 330	- UP
Excellent	90% - 325	- 315
Very Good	80% - 310	- 295
Good	70% - 290	- 270
Average	60% - 265	- 240
Marginal	50% - 235	- 220

RANKING .... **PARALLEL SQUAT**

Superior	100% - 540	- UP
Excellent	90% - 535	- 520
Very Good	80% - 515	- 500
Good	70% - 495	- 470
Average	60% - 465	- 430
Marginal	50% - 425	- 380

RANKING .... **VERTICAL JUMP**

Superior	100% - 30"	- UP
Excellent	90% - 29.5	29.0
Very Good	80% - 28.5	27.5
Good	70% - 27.0	26.0
Average	60% - 25.5	24.0
Marginal	50% - 23.5	21.0

RANKING .... **STAND JUMP**

Superior	100% - 9'4"	- UP
Excellent	90% -9'3"-	8'10"
Very Good	80% -8'9"-	8'6"
Good	70% -8'5"-	8'2"
Average	60% -8'1"-	7'10"
Marginal	50% -7'9"-	7'3"

RANKING .... **40-YARD SPRINT**

Superior	100% - 4.80	- LESS
Excellent	90% - 4.81	- 4.90
Very Good	80% - 4.91	- 5.00
Good	70% - 5.01	- 5.10
Average	60% - 5.11	- 5.25
Marginal	50% - 5.26	- 5.35

ANTHROPOMETRIC
SPRING SCORE - FALL GOAL

HEIGHT ...... _____

WEIGHT...... _____ - _____

% FAT .... _____ - _____

STRENGTH
SPRING SCORE - % VALUE - FALL GOAL

BENCH .... _____ - _____ - _____

CLEAN........ _____ - _____ - _____

SQUAT .... _____ - _____ - _____

AVG. .... _____ - _____ - _____

POWER/SPEED
SPRING SCORE - % VALUE - FALL GOAL

V/JUMP ...... _____ - _____ - _____

S/JUMP ...... _____ - _____ - _____

40 YDS .... _____ - _____ - _____

AVG. .... _____ - _____ - _____

STRENGTHS
1. _____
2. _____
3. _____

LIMITATIONS
1. _____
2. _____
3. _____

WEAKNESS AREAS
1. _____
2. _____
3. _____

AREAS TO IMPROVE
1. _____
2. _____
3. _____

Chapter 12

OFFENSIVE LINE DRILLS

By
Jimmy Ray Stephens
University of Florida
1998

We have the reputation of being a passing team, but I think the running game gives us the balance to be successful. Keeping that balance in the offense is important. We try to keep it simple in the running game. We have to spend so much time with pass protection that the running game has to be simple.

The offensive line is based on a lot of repetition. Repetition is the mother of learning. We repeat things so many times that we try to reduce things down to habit. We want to be able to execute without having to think so much. When the offensive lineman is thinking a lot, it slows down his aggressiveness.

I try to go to the pro camps in the areas to stay on top of the new techniques and drills. The fundamentals generally stay the same, but I like to keep abreast of what is going on. Sometimes you have to be creative and come up with your own drills. Most drills are borrowed from people who have done them for years and years.

What I'm going to show you is an offensive line teaching progression. This is where I start out every year in the spring and fall. Never assume that your guys already know what you want them to know. We have guys who are fifth-year seniors and have been in this program for four years. We still start from scratch every year. The progression is split, stance, approach, contact, and follow-through. That goes for run blocking as well as pass blocking. Everything we do is pretty much a three-step approach and after that it is effort. There are different types of contact. If we are at the point of attack, we are using punch and hand blocking. There are times when we use the flipper in the contact. When we are the post man on a double team, we use the flipper. We use the flipper or forearm on the back side in the scoop block. We use a rip upper cut when the lineman is farther removed from the play. That would be like a sweep moving away from the lineman. That requires a flatter angle coming down inside.

Follow-through is nothing but effort. We try to finish every drill with a shove. It might be that little extra shove that gets the defender off balance and causes him to stumble or arm tackle the runner. We teach our one-on-one run blocks first. Everything else works off of that. We have play-side zone blocks and backside zone blocks, We work at every position about the same as far as technique. We work our guys in two-on-two situations as much as possible. We have the double-team block both play side and back side and finally the fold block. We don't fold block much. Because of the shades and slants that we are getting now, most everything is zone blocking.

We have our pattern blocking, which is the counter gap and trap blocking. That is zone and pattern blocking all rolled into one.

In pass blocking we have one-on-one blocking. We have the position and contact phases. We have counter moves for various pass-rush moves, in that we have two-on-two blocking, which involves the switching games. The last thing is our pass protection schemes.

Real quickly let me talk about our practice schedule. I'll show you an example of a Tuesday and Wednesday schedule when we are in full gear. On Monday and Thursday we have a 50-minute block for special teams. Fortunately for me none of my guys are in those groups except for field goal and extra point. That gives me a 50-minute block that I can go back over fundamentals of the one-on-one block and things I need to work on.

This is a typical schedule. After stretching we kick PAT's and field goals. We have a team takeoff period and then go to an individual period. It usually lasts about 25-30 minutes. During this time I try to do run-blocking fundamentals. After the individual period, we go into a seven-on-seven period. That is an inside run period live against the defense. It is a full-speed contact drill. That is about the only full-speed drill we get during the week after the season starts. After that period we take a break.

From the break the rest of the squad goes to some form of the kicking game. I go by myself and work on pass-blocking techniques and fundamentals. Next is when coach Spurrier goes to his pass skeleton drill. As you can see there is more time allotted to the passing game than there is in the running game. During that time I work one-on-

one, two-on-two, and five-on-four pass protection. We work that full speed against the defense. After that we go into a team drill. That is the way we do things on Tuesday and Wednesday.

Thursday is a review day. We spend a lot of time on special teams. During that time I review all the blocking we expect to see during the coming week.

What I would like to do now is get into the drill tape. As we go along I'll point out some coaching techniques and points. The first thing we do is to go through the low ropes. These are four inches high. We are trying to keep our feet as close to the ground as possible. We want the body lean and have our feet and arms working together. We want as fast a turnover as possible.

The next thing we do is go to an agility period. We use the carioca drill. That is where we turn sideways and work our feet in front and behind one another. We try to stay low and use rapid movement. We don't want to cover ground. We want to see how many we can get in within the 10 yards we work. That is a loosening-up drill.

The next drill we do is called the "DEMEANOR DRILL." Basically, all it is is a two-point wave drill. We are working on wide base, straight back, head up, and good foot movement. What we are looking for are feet close to the ground, retaining the wide base, and good ground coverage. They never want their heels to click together in this movement. If the right foot moves six inches, the left foot should move six inches. The closer the feet are to the ground the quicker he can redirect his movement. We move them forward, backward, and sideways. We want them to feel like they have a steel rod right down their spine. We want the weight balanced. We don't want it on the outside of the feet, back on their heels, or up on the balls of the feet. We try to balance with the whole foot on the ground. We want the weight on the insteps.

The next thing we go to in the fundamental work is the first step. We take very little first steps. We make contact on the second step. We work the lateral or bucket step as a first step. The first step depends upon the alignment of the defender. The 45-degree angle step is called a lead step. The elbows come to the rib cage on the takeoff. The hands must come up quickly. We don't want to bring our hands back to the hips.

On the offensive line field we have painted on the ground 5-yard squares. We have seven squares across the field and about four squares deep. We do our drills in these 5-yard squares. They have space to work without running over each other and we can work them all at one time. There is nothing that irritates me more than having one guy working and everyone else standing there watching. We try to keep them all moving at the same time. We try to do everything off a line. The center is the only guy who will have some-one right on him. Everyone else will have about a foot and a half of the neutral zone between him and the defense. We try to get off the ball so we can recognize slants and stunts up front. Also, it helps us get our second step on the ground. We want the second step on the ground when contact is made.

Let's go through these first steps. THE BUCKET STEP is a drop step with width. We are trying to gain width, depth, and to open the hips up. We want our hips and shoulders open to the target. Sometimes you have to lose ground to gain position. One thing that we never want to do is "Move to Move." That means adding a false step.

In this drill we lay hand shields down on the ground to indicate align-ments of defenders. The offensive line is going to work on footwork for our inside zone play. The hand shields can be head up, inside eye, or outside eye. Those are the only places a defender can be. The fist step for the play-side people is a slide step. The second step goes just inside the near foot of the defender. We try not to cross over so we don't lose our base. The third step is a width step or position step.

The backside people are working on backside scoop angles and steps. The backside guard's angle is tighter than the backside tackle's. The guard is using a flipper and trying to get his eyes on the inside armpit of the defender. He uses the same flipper and foot so he has his foot on the ground as he delivers the punch. The tackle is going to cross over into the gap and try to get a rip up in the pit position, just like a defensive lineman pass rushing. On the back side, contact is made on the second step, also. Most of the time, unless the defender is really slow, the backside cutoff block will end up in a drive block on a 45-degree angle inside. That lets the back cut all the way back if he has to. Remember, you may have to lose ground to gain position. If I am a backside tackle trying to cut off a 3 Technique, my first step can't be upfield. If it is, the next step will be farther upfield or he will have to cross over. If he does that he loses his base. He uses a bucket step to open his hips and loses a little ground. The next step allows him to get his head in front of the 3 Technique.

On a double-team block the post man has to step with his inside foot to protect the inside gap. This is the counter gap play. Basically, everyone is blocking down. But it doesn't make sense for the man who is covered to take off inside to block a backside linebacker. He posts on the double team and comes off for the linebacker when the double team gets to linebacker depth. The fist step for a head up to four-eye defender is inside. If the defender is in an outside shade, the step is more upfield. That is to keep the defender from splitting the double team. The first step is inside, the second step is upfield for the contact, and the third step is the width step.

The drive man on the double-team first step is an open step. That opens his hips toward the target. There are three types of down blocks. It is important to know that because the defender is going to read differently on them and the target or landmark will change. Most defenders are going to read on the run and attack through the V of the offensive blocker's neck. On the down block on the double team, the landmark is farther upfield. The landmark is the near hip of the defender. If there is a down block without a double team the down block has to be a flatter angle, because the defender is going down with the offensive linemen as he goes inside. The landmark becomes the defender's inside armpit or far hip. If the down block comes with a guard pull, there is a different reaction by the defender. The defender will work lateral with the pulling guard and the landmark becomes the defender's near armpit. The angle a down blocker takes depends on the assignment of the offensive linemen inside the down block.

The other thing the down blocker must consider is how the defender is playing. He has to find out if the defender is penetrating or reading. We feel that our people play better if they have their outside foot back in their stances. That is particularly true in pass protection. Therefore we teach right- and left-handed stances. People on the right will have their right hand down and right foot back. People on the left will have their left hand down and their left foot back.

The next thing we work on is a 5-yard pull technique. We drop step and pull around the bags. The coaching point is coming around the bag. As the player turns upfield, he drives the inside arm down. That keeps the center of gravity low as they turn upfield.

The next thing you'll see is the one-step punch. We teach the punch. We hit the bottom three knuckles on the hand punching up and through. After the punch we get our hands in the fit position under the breastplate of the pads. We punch, arch the back, and roll the hips.

The next drill you will see is the FIT DRILL. We take the offensive blocker and defender and lock them into a fitted block. We put the hairline where it is supposed to be on contact. Then we try to get the good demeanor. The back is arched, the weight is flat-footed, rolled to the inside on the insteps, and the hands are behind the back. We do this without using our hands. If the blocker gets his weight on the balls of his feet, he gets more horizontal and lower in the blocking scheme. In high school I'm sure people use more of a horizontal thrust. In college and the pro level there is a lot more vertical thrust. We are blocking up higher, because of the pass protection. The main thing is to get the hat on a defender and stick on him. Don't lose your block. When you get up on the balls of the feet you are getting overextended with a flat back. If the defender steps right or left, the blocker will fall forward and lose his block. We feel the days of knocking guys off the ball are over. The guy across from you will be on scholarship, too.

What we are looking for is a stalemate. We are coming off and moving our feet like crazy. At some point in time the defender has to drop step to try to get off the block and make the tackle. That is when the offensive lineman finishes the block and puts the defender on his back.

In the no-hands drill we want the defender to move right and left so the blocker has to keep his feet moving and maintain contact.

After we go with no hands, we use the hands. We still fit in, but now the hands are fitted into position. The defensive man tries to completely stalemate the offensive blocker. That forces the offensive blocker to push out of the stalemate and accelerate his feet at contact while maintaining a wide base. We want the defense to take a right or left movement, so the blocker can practice staying with his block and finishing.

After we do that we put it all together. We slide step, second step and punch, widen step and drive, and finish the block. Most of our drive blocks are up in drive angle blocks. Very seldom will someone drive someone straight back off the ball. Everyone lines up at angles and that is the way we drive them.

Now we put them in a linebacker drill and go over their foot movement. When everyone was covered they used the slide step as their first step. With linebacker coverage, they use a bucket step. The lineman gets a one-handed read to the down man who is one hole over. He keeps his eyes on the linebacker. The lineman takes a bucket step and his second step is a crossover step. His crossover step has to be kept underneath the lineman's body. If it isn't, his pads turn too flat to the sideline and he will never get them square to go up on the linebacker. If the linebacker fast flows and the down man slants inside, the offensive lineman goes from a one-handed read to two hands on the down man. On the third step, the lineman has to make a decision. He is either locking on to the slanting down man or climbing up to the linebacker. After he gets to the second level with the linebacker his technique goes back to what he did if he were covered. He punches, locks on, arches his back, rolls his hips and accelerates his feet. The finish is the last thing he does.

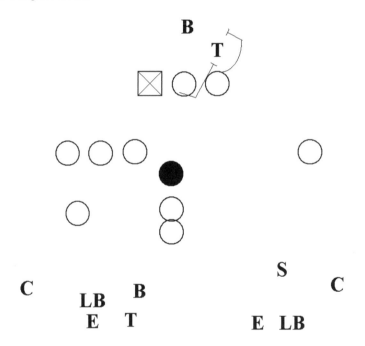

The covered man starts off with a two-handed punch. If the defender locks him and works outside he continues to block him. If the defender starts to move inside on the slant, the guard inside has one hand on him. The covered man has two hands on him. They end up in a double team on the slanting tackle. The guard goes from a one-handed feel to a two-handed drive block on the slanting tackle. The offensive tackle goes from a two-handed punch and drive to a one-handed press-off to go to the linebacker who is flowing across the top. All zone plays start out as an inside-out double team. Try to stay away from long steps. We want short steps all the time. The harder the punch the more the hips will roll up underneath. If you don't get a punch with the upper body, you end up leaning on one another with no power.

Their techniques are done by all linemen and tight ends on the zone play. If the uncovered man was the tackle and the covered man was the tight end, they would do the drill just like a guard and tackle. The tackle would bucket set, half cross step, and take a wide step with the one-handed read on the man over the end. The end would use the slide step, two-hand punch on the second step, and widen on the third step. If the man over the tight end slanted, the tackle would go from one to two hands and get into an angle drive block. The tight end would go from a two-handed punch to a one-handed press-off up to linebacker depth. If the defensive end locked the tight end's block and started to work outside, the tight end would continue his angle drive block. The tackle on his third step would release the down man and climb up to linebacker depth to take the linebacker.

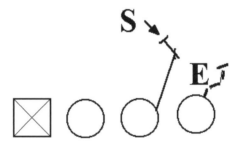

In our drill we line the defender outside and lock on or slant. When we line the defender inside we do both. On Monday we do all of our one-on-one drills. On Tuesday and Wednesday is when we do these two-on-one zone blocks. The center is the only man who makes contact on the first step. If he is in a double-team situation with his right guard, he steps off with his near foot to the guard. His flipper and head remain on the backside number of the defender. If the post man on a double team sets the post with his hands, he will never get them off to pick up a run-through by the linebacker. His eyes are on the linebacker. The guard steps off with a slide step to the inside. If the linebacker runs through on the back side, the center comes off and blocks him. If the linebacker flows over the top, the center has to helmet adjust and slip to the play side to get his head across the block. The guard is coming off for the linebacker.

Let's get into our pass sets. If the guard has a man head up on him, he is going to take a short inside slide step. That is to protect the inside. If the tackle has a guy head up on him, he is going to step inside and off the ball a little. If there is an inside shade and that is his responsibility, he has to set heavy down inside and move both feet. That is called a two-step set. He has to get to a frontal position and square the man up. The contact will be off the inside foot. If there is a tight outside shade, we use a one-step set. If there is a loose 3 Technique, we use a two-step set. The lineman wants to set so that his body is between the defender and the quarterback's pocket. The center and guard should keep his pads square at all times. The tackle will have a slight turn with his pads toward the sideline, but should never have his pad turned all the way toward the sideline.

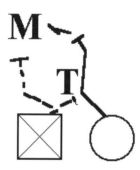

The thing we emphasize is get set quick, get the hands up quickly, with the head and shoulders back. They always keep their post foot up and the set foot back. They keep that stagger to help them stay low. If the blocker doesn't get his second foot down, he gets too spread out in his base. The defender will beat him upfield and the only choice the offensive lineman has is to bail out and cross over. We have to be balanced. The more foot you've got on the ground the more balance you have.

During our pass set drill, we also work on our draw set. We inside set, punch him up, pivot, and turn. We incorporate that into this drill.

Chapter 13

OFFENSIVE LINE DRILLS AND TECHNIQUES

By
Chris Vagotis
University of Louisville
1990

Let me talk about offensive line play. My philosophy is a lot different now than it was when I was coaching in high school. We can recruit in college and most of you can't in high school. So I know where you are coming from. If something fits into my program I am going to put it in the program. I am not going to give you something that you cannot do. I am not going to talk about running our whole offense, which consists of close to possibly 120 plays against multiple defensive fronts. I want to give you something you can use.

In high school I would take my best lineman and put him at center. Anyone can learn how to snap the ball. That good lineman may not want to snap, but he can learn to snap the football. We tell the center to take the ball and grip the ball around the right stripe and tell him to squeeze it hard. We want him to lift the ball up to the Quarterback's hand with the laces the way you want them.

We want the center to make a natural arc with his arm as he brings the ball straight up. "Set-Hike. Set-Hike." That is all there is to it. Most centers want to throw the ball back. A good drill to check to see if the center is getting the ball back is for the Quarterback to let the ball hit his top hand and then Drop to the turf. If the ball goes forward as it hits the ground, it means the center is too short on the snap. If the ball goes backward, the center is lifting the ball too deep. The ball should drop straight down to the turf.

We teach the center to snap with both hands on the ball. He snaps, and moves his feet. He snaps and steps; snaps and steps.

In high school football the center is the most important position. In college our open-side tackle must be our best athlete because he has to block the outside rusher. If you throw the ball a lot, that is true. It all depends on what you run on offense. If you run the Veer take the big hogs and put them at the guards. If the defense you face covers your guards, you should put your best players at guards.

We do not use any drills that do not correlate with what we do in a game. We do not do Up-Downs. All drills we do are directly related to what we do in a game. We do incidental drills in our off-season conditioning program such as the Wave Drill. To me, those types of drills you use for punishment.

I. **FOUR PLASTIC CONES** — 7-yard square. We can backpedal, shuffle, and pull right and left on this drill.

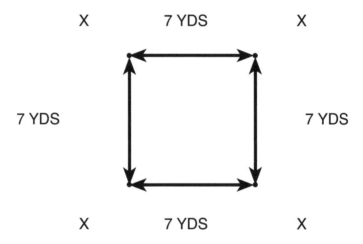

DRILLS

A. Shuffle to first cone and sprint through next cone.

B. Step Around—Stance step around—touch cone—eyeball coach. Used for pulling guards. Eyeball linebacker.

C. Backpedal—pivot—sprint—sprint. We get in a three-point stance. When he starts to backpedal he wants to punch with his hands. We do not want him to take a hitch step; that is taking a step forward. He is like a boxer punching a bag as he kicks back.

D. Scramble Stance: Sprint to coach, scramble to next cone.

Sled 50 Pass Pro Stance—Frontal on sled—lock out hands—head held back.

Off Set Rt.—Lt.—Scramble low to knee—Aiming Points—six inches outside knee, three inches high.

Off Set Rt.—Lt.—Reach outside breast plate.

Drive—Flat Back—Short, choppy steps—Head up

Low Drive to Crotch—High Drive to V of neck

II. **BAGS AND BOARDS**—six beveled boards 12' x 1'x 2" thick with a T-board 3' x 2" x 2". The boards are painted with lines to represent hands of down man and linebacker.

BOARD DRILLS

A. Drive vs. down man; linebackers

B. Scramble vs. down man

C. Turn vs. down man; linebackers

BAG DRILLS

A. Drive with bags

B. Off Set Rt./Lt.—Scramble low to knee.

C. Off Set Rt./Lt.—Reach to breast plate

D. Trap Technique

E. Trap Technique—Step around first force log

CHUTE DRILLS

A. Drive

B. Reach Right and Left

C. Scramble Right and Left

D. Trap Right and Left

The purpose of the drill is to keep the shoulders down, back straight, and all five men coming off the ball simultaneously.

I do not believe in using the shoulder block. I think the shoulder block causes more neck, shoulder, and spinal injuries than anything else in football. If you don't do the shoulder block perfectly, you open up the neck area to the defense. I believe in aiming the hat in there and sticking the hands inside and knocking the man off the ball. Take no mercy on the defensive man. He will gore you if he gets you down. Knock him down. Do it legally, but put him away.

On our alignment and stance we are no different than most teams. Our Offensive Line is in a three-point stance with a toe-to-heel relationship. Our Halfbacks and Fullback shift from the I to a finished position on the command of set. They get to a three-point stance with their feet square unless the play called is to be run from the I or if the play called is a Split play and the snap count is on a first or second count. Our X and Z receivers are in a three-point stance.

On our splits our guards should have a 24-inch split from the center. Our tackles should have a 36-inch split from the guard. Our tight end is 36 inches split from the tackle on his base alignment. He could also be in a flex set. Here is a very important coaching point. Our guards line up on the *heels* of the center. The tackles line up on the *hand* of the guards. The tight end lines up on the *hands* of the tackles.

HOLE NUMBERING SYSTEM

A. Holes are numbered through offensive linemen.

B. All plays ending in an EVEN number go to the right.

C. All plays ending in an ODD number go to the left.

PRO RIGHT

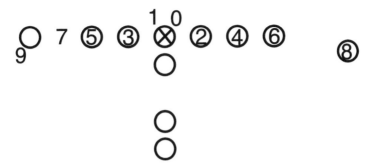

PRO LEFT

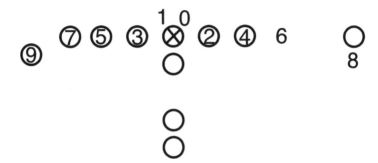

We cut the center in half and give him the 0 and 1 numbers. If we called a 32 play the 3 back would carry the ball through the 2 hole. We are very simple. We count everyone on defense from the inside to the outside. Against the 50 defense the Linebacker is number 1, the Tackle is number 2, the End is number 3, and the Rover is number 4.

We have alignments and techniques so we can communicate with our players. We have three areas for each alignment. If the noseguard is in an 0 technique, he would be in a plus (+) technique if he shades to the tight end. If he shades away from the tight end he is in a minus (-) technique. The guard has a 2, 1, and 3 technique. The tackle has a 5 and a 7 technique. Our end has a 6, 8, and 9 technique. We use this to communicate where the defense is playing more than anything else.

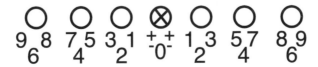

I want to cover some basic blocks that we use. I will cover the technique, when we use the block, and how we teach the block.

DRIVE BLOCK

We must have movement on the block.

WHEN: Ball is coming up your butt and the play is a quick-hitting play.

Examples: 20/21 for the center; 12/13 for the guards.

HOW: Sprint out of stance taking a six-inch step with your play-side foot in the direction that puts you square to the defender. Your feet at the point of contact should be exactly square to his. The aiming point for the rivets should be through his crotch; your forearms should make contact on his thigh pads. We must fight to maintain our *flat* back. After contact we must maintain a wide base and drive through the defender with quick, short steps. Coaching Point: Imagine a point 5 yards behind the defender where your rivets and his butt should land. *Run through defenders*. Drive to and through the defender.

POINTS IN THE DRIVE BLOCK

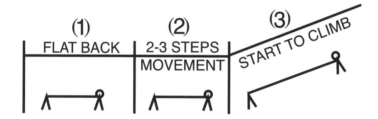

When coaching the Drive Block and making corrections make your linemen aware of the mistakes of the blocks. Ask the players watching what the blocker did incorrectly or correctly.

TURN BLOCK

This is basically the same as the Drive Block, only higher. We must have movement.

WHEN: Ball is being handed off up your butt to the second back on a slow-developing play.

Examples: Guard vs. 3 tech. on 14; Tackle vs. 5 tech. on 34; Center vs. nose on Draw - 0.

HOW: Take a six-inch step with your play-side foot in a direction that puts you square to the defender. Your feet at the point of contact should be exactly square to his. The aiming point of your rivets should be the "V" in his jersey. Your fists should make contact in his breast-plate. Even though we are blocking slightly uphill, we still want two steps worth of movement before we try to turn him in either direction we can get him to go.

SCRAMBLE BLOCK

WHEN: The ball is going inside or outside of you on a quick-hitting play that has a chance to cut back. Basically for plays called inside of our guards.

HOW: Sprint out of stance with flat back. Just before contact, dip and explode. Aiming point for the play side should be six inches outside of the defender's play-side foot. The flatness of your angle will be determined by the width of the defender's alignment. Aim your rivets six inches outside and three inches above his play-side knee. Try and split his crotch with your back and work your butt between him and the ball.

Coaching Point: Scramble with him at least two steps, then give an upward thrust with the head and body. If you feel you lost the block, get back on your feet and get to the play.

VEER BLOCK

This block is for the guard and tackle. They block through the first man inside.

WHEN: As the rule calls for it. We do not use this block much now. The guard doesn't veer if covered (unless the game plan dictates).

HOW: 1. WHEN VEERING FOR MAN OFF LINE OF SCRIMMAGE

(Example: Tackle on 20 vs. 50) You sprint out of your stance, aiming your inside foot six inches inside of the defender's outside foot. Aim your rivets six inches outside and three inches above his play-side knee. Split his crotch with your inside fist and reach for the ground behind his play-side foot with your outside fist.

Coaching point: If you miss him, look inside for the next Linebacker or Lineman in pursuit. If the Tackle slants across your face, take him down with you.

2. WHEN VEERING THROUGH MAN ON LINE OF SCRIMMAGE

Example 1: Guard on nose

Example 2: Tackle on Eagle tackle

We aim our inside foot six inches outside of the defender's play-side foot, expecting the guard or center to widen him at least that far. We take a zone step (lateral) over and up, driving our inside shoulder through his play-side hip, trying to turn him over to the man scrambling him while we work to veer block the next man inside, usually a Linebacker. We should only stay with the man we are Veering on if he gains a head-up position on us.

REACH BLOCK

WHEN: Same theory as the Scramble Block except higher. It is used when the second back has the ball on a slow-developing play that has a chance to cut back. So we must maintain contact a lot longer.

Examples: Back side of Draw 2 or 3; back side of 34 for tackle; the onside on 38 for tackle.

HOW: Sprint out of stance aiming your play-side foot six inches outside of the defender's play-side foot. (Try to make him think it is a Turn or Drive Block.) Aim your rivets for his play-side breastplate. (Your angle will be determined by the width of his alignment.) Aim your fist for his armpits. Try to make him fight pressure of the drive block, then slip your back shoulder trying to get outside position on him.

Coaching Point: The wider he is the less you can disguise the reach block. If he is too wide, make fold call or try to scramble him.

Finally, I want to cover our Sprint Draw Play-Action Passing Game. The first question we must answer is this: Why the sprint draw play-action pass? We run it for these three reasons:

1. To help set up the Sprint Draw Run.

2. Gives us seven-man protection (can stop all blitzes except a Perimeter Blitz).

3. Can be thrown against all coverage.

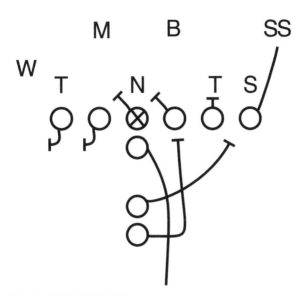

SPRINT DRAW PROTECTION

OT—TURNBACK

OG—TURNBACK: CP – if you and tackle are both covered - block straight

C—TURNBACK: ALERT STRAIGHT CALL

BG—TURNBACK: ALERT STRAIGHT CALL

BT—TURNBACK: ALERT STRAIGHT CALL

Y—ROUTE

X—ROUTE

Z—ROUTE

FB—BLOCK #3 CONTROLLED AGGRESSIVE

HG—SPRINT DRAW FAKE: Block play-side Linebacker. If Linebacker is on the line of scrimmage check Mike to Will. You are responsible for perimeter pressure strong.

QB—SPRINT DRAW FAKE: PLAY-ACTION TECHNIQUE.

Now let's look at three passes.

ROUTE #1: Can be thrown vs. ANY coverage.

1. This play is designed to vertically stretch the center of the field.

2. After play-action fake, QUARTERBACK sets up 9–10 yards behind strongside guard.

A. VS. 3-DEEP STRONGSIDE ZONE COVERAGE:

1. QB may look to hit TE in front of the weakside end who has taken a straight pass drop underneath number 1 (split end) because number 2 and number 3 (FB and TB) have gone strong side. OTHERWISE:

2. QB picks up Weak Safety after fake. If Weak Safety has settled down in the middle of the field, the QUARTERBACK will look to throw the deep post over the middle of the field to the split end.

3. If the WS has run to take away the deep post the QUARTERBACK will look to throw the Square-In to the Flanker or the flat route by the TB with a high/low distribution off the SS. (Hopefully, we have held the strong inside linebacker with the fake long enough so he is not a factor getting underneath the flanker.)

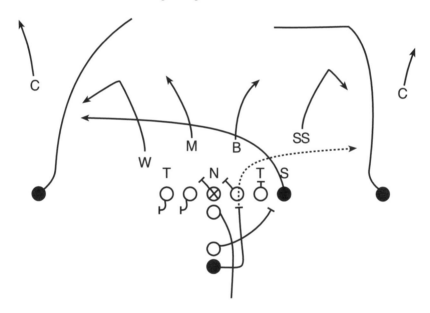

B. VS. 2-DEEP ZONE COVERAGE

1. Most likely the TE is not open because either the weakside corner or linebacker is in the flat waiting on the TE after the jam on the split end.

2. We do not generally think of going to the deep post with the WS and Strong Safety each covering one half of the field.

3. Our thinking is to create a vertical stretch on the strong side of the field with the flanker and the tailback. (This time against the strongside outside linebacker who covers the slot in a weakside rotation.)

C. VS. MAN-TO-MAN COVERAGE

1. Forget play fake; take five-step drop.

2. Look to TE first being chased.

3. Look to Split End on deep post since WS is out of middle of the field.

4. Look to TB being chased if strongside linebacker does not blitz.

ROUTE 2: Can be thrown vs. ANY coverage.

1. This play is designed to vertically stretch the weak corner or weak outside linebacker in the weakside flat area.

2. After play-action fake QUARTERBACK sets up 9–10 yards behind the strongside guard.

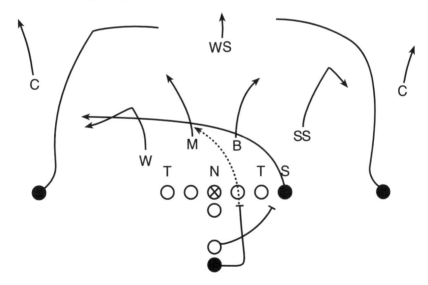

A. VS. 3-DEEP STRONGSIDE COVERAGE

1. QUARTERBACK will look to high-low the weakside linebacker in the weak flat.

2. C/P: If weakside outside linebacker is between the TE and SE, the QUARTERBACK should look to hit the TE.

3. If the weakside outside linebacker jumps the TE, the QUARTER-BACK will look to hit the SE one-on-one with the weakside corner.

4. If both TE and SE are covered, look to hit the TB hooked up.

B. VS. 2-DEEP ZONE COVERAGE

1. QUARTERBACK will look to high-low the weakside flat occupied by the weakside corner or weakside outside linebacker who is responsible for jamming the split end.

2. If the defender designed to jam and occupy the flat settles back in the deep flat, the QUARTERBACK should hit the TE.

3. If the defender designed to jam and occupy the flat (Will or Corner) does jam and looks to pick up the TE as he tries to invade the defender's zone, the QUARTERBACK should look to hit the comeback run by the split end off the man defending the deep weakside one half.

C. VS. MAN-TO-MAN COVERAGE

1. Forget play-action fake.

2. Fake five-step drop and look to hit TE being chased.

3. If TE is not going to be open, go seven steps and hit the SE on a comeback.

4. Note: May get Flanker on Post with weak safety out of the middle of field.

ROUTE 3: Can be thrown vs. ANY coverage.

1. This play is designed to vertically stretch the center of the field.

2. After play-action fake QUARTERBACK sets up 9-10 yards behind strongside guard.

A. VS. 3-DEEP STRONGSIDE ZONE COVERAGE.

1. QUARTERBACK may look to hit TE in front of weakside end who has taken a straight pass drop underneath number 1 (split end) because number 2 and number 3 (FB and TB) have gone strongside. OTHERWISE:

2. QUARTERBACK will pick up WS after play-action fake if WS has settled down in the middle of the field to the flanker.

3. If the WS has run to take away the deep post, the QUARTER-BACK looks to throw the Square-In to the SE or the Check-Down to the TB who has settled approximately 6 yards deep over the original position of the weak linebacker. (With distribution of the flanker on a Square-In and TB on a Check-Down we hope to get high-low separation off the weak linebacker.)

4. We hope the run fake holds the linebacker so he doesn't affect Square-In.

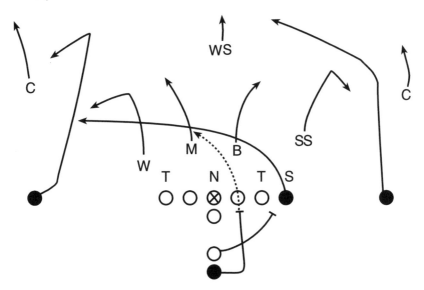

B. VS. 2-DEEP ZONE COVERAGE

1. More than likely the TE will not be open; either weakside corner or outside linebacker will be in the flat waiting on the TE after jam on the split end.

2. We do not generally think of going to the deep post with the WS and SS each covering deep half of the field.

3. Our thinking is to create a vertical stretch on the weakside inside linebacker with the SE and TB.

C. VS. MAN-TO-MAN COVERAGE

1. Forget play fake, take five-step drop.

2. Look to TE first being chased.

3. Look to flanker on deep post, since WS is out of middle of the field.

Chapter 14

COACHING THE OFFENSIVE LINE

By
Art Valero
University of Louisville
1998

I'm not going to talk too much about our basic offense and how we go about doing things and what we look for. We will let anyone who wants to see us come out and watch us on film and see what we are doing. Then you can figure us out, because it is a very, very complex offense. We are a One-Back offense. And unlike most One-Back offenses they do certain things in terms of protecting the passer and running the football, and that is all they do. They don't have the answers for all of those questions that come up with the receivers.

We have a lot of answers for those problems that always arise for a One-Back scheme. Our feeling is this: We will spread you out offensively by formation. We are going to spread you out and make you declare. We make you decide if you are going to play with three true linebackers, or if you are going to play a Nickel scheme, where you try to change those guys who are too big to be safeties into linebackers. If you are going to get those types of guys, we feel like we have wide receivers who are better than you are in terms of running routes. When we come back into our One-Back Set, we look for spreading you out. We basically have a rule of thumb. If you have one linebacker in the box, we are going to run the ball. If you have two linebackers in there, we are going to throw the ball. So, the perception may be that we are a throwing football team and we are going to throw every down. Well, that is not true. We are a 50-50 football team. Unlike some coordinator's comments, where they may not be sure if they want to run the ball or they want to throw the ball, we want you to play us one way or the other. Then our identity will come out in terms of either shortening this football game up and running it at you, or we are going to shorten this football game up and create big plays and throw the ball. We would prefer you play Nickel against us. That means you have got your fifth-worst football player on the field in the secondary trying to cover our wideouts. Not only is he your fifth-worst pass defender, like most defensive backs, he is probably your eighth- or ninth-worst running defender. So that puts it all back into our hands.

When we talk about formations, we will go balance into a 2-by-2 set that we will get into a majority of the time, although we don't necessarily like it because it doesn't create any unbalanced situations. We like trips, which means we have the tight end into the boundary with three receivers to the one side, or we will go with the tight end to the field with two receivers and a single receiver into the boundary. So we are going to try to spread you out from a One-Back standpoint. To us, blasphemy is when you put more than one guy back there in the backfield. When you put more than one guy back there what ends up happening is this, he just brings another defender into the box. That is something that we do not want to happen. Because now you are asking this: instead of those six guys blocking for that running back, now you are asking for six guys, plus a guy who may not be one of your better blockers to block the extra man. We would rather spread you out and then go about our business.

Our system of football is 50-50 run and pass, and that is our identity. We want to be able to do both. The keys to our success on offense and, since 1990, this offense has been ranked in the top 10 each of the years. Not only by throwing the ball, but by running it. So we feel like we have got a good system of football. In order for us to win on offense, there are basically five things that we need to adhere to all of the time.

Number 1 is that we are going to run the ball first and foremost. It is our responsibility as a coaching staff, it is our responsibility as an offensive line, to make sure that we run the football. Number 2, we are going to throw the Three-Step Drop or what we call our 90 passing game. Those are our short routes. We let our wideouts make big plays off of that. Our third thing that we are going to do is empty the backfield. So basically we've got five eligible receivers going out. We put the ball in our quarterback's hands and let him make something happen. Those routes may be Three-Step Drop type routes, or Five-Step Drop type routes. We are going to spread you out horizontally so we can stretch you vertically. The fourth thing that we have got to do is make play-action passes work. That is where we get big plays. The fifth thing we do is throw our "80" or our Five-Step Drops. What we want to do when we throw Five-Step Drops is to throw them when we want to, not when we have to. A lot teams want to drop back and go five steps every single time. The one thing from an offensive line standpoint that they seem to forget is that the quarterback doesn't move very often. He sets in the same spot and that puts extra pressure on your people up front. So we talk about it as a staff in terms of throwing Five-Step Drop routes; we take the offensive linemen into consideration and the job that they have to do.

A couple of things I want to talk about real quick just to start this thing out. Again, I'm not going to talk much about our general overall scheme. I want to talk about what I like, and that is the offensive line play. The skills each football player learns throughout his life, in grade school, in high school, college or the NFL, are skills he has developed over his lifetime. Let me give you an example. Say you are a fourth-grader. You go for recess. What is the first thing you do? You and your buddies split up sides and go play football. You are working on skills as a young person that entire time. You work on throwing the ball. Now, not everyone can be a quarterback, but nevertheless you work on those skills of throwing the football. You work on catching the ball. You work on running the ball after the catch. You work on pass coverage. You work on tackling, you work on all of the different things and skills that we all as coaches like out of our athletes. But there is one major skill development that is never brought into the picture. That is either blocking, or if you are a defensive guy, getting rid of the block and going on to make the tackle. Not too many fourth graders ever go out and say, "Hey Johnny, let's go work on our football techniques. You rush the passer and let me protect the passer today." So those are things that never ever happen as a young man. Those are skills that you never learn. So what happens, once you get into junior high or middle school, or high school, your coach says, "You are an offensive linemen, or you are a center today." What is the kid thinking? "Oh my gosh, what did I do wrong? What did I do to deserve this?" Then he starts thinking, "All my buddies are catching passes and getting their names in the paper and here I am, because I'm slightly overweight, and I cannot move very well, and I have very few skills, so what do I get to do?" Well, that happens all of the time. Those fat kids, my heart goes out to them. Once upon a time when I was young, I was a fat kid. So I got stuck playing with my hand down. Those guys who create that situation that allows everybody else to get into the limelight are the guys who make your offense go. Each of those skills that you have to do are the ones that allow you to have success on offense, whether it be running the football or throwing the football.

What we try to do is this. There are four must things that an offensive line must do. We talk about it in boxing terms. This puts everything into perspective as far as what I am looking for in an offensive linemen and what we try to get out of them. That term is this: "If you kill the body, the head must die." I heard a boxer talk about that one time and it is perfect for offensive line play. It simply means this: If you can work on a defender's body and you can beat on him, and beat on him, and make it a physical part of the game from the first quarter through the third quarter, then in the fourth quarter, his head will die. He will give up. He will not want it anymore. And those are things that we are constantly striving to do. When people say, "Yeah, you are 50-50," this is what we say. We are going to make running the football a major emphasis, and we are going to make being physical a part of protecting the passer a major emphasis. Because we are going to try to work on your body.

The first thing we have got to live and die with is this. I tell them if they do not have an attitude right now, then you've got to go out and find an attitude, right now. Our attitude is this: We take no crap from nobody, no time, nowhere, period. It does not matter if it be on the practice field, whether that is during a game, or whether that is on campus, or downtown. But, unlike other positions, we have to be smart about it. Sure, if we go out and get in a little scuffle during practice, that is just two guys competing. Our job at practice is this, and you may not want your guys to do this: If one of us gets in it, we are all in it, because I have to know somebody covers my back. Now you may get punished, and you may have to run after practice. It is just like when you were a little kid and mom bakes a brand-new cake. She tells you not to touch it until dinner. You sneak a piece after school. You may get in trouble for it, but it was sweet going down. That is a thing that we make sure we do. We want our offensive linemen to make sure they protect each other and protect the rest of the offense.

The second thing we have to do is technique. My firm belief is that you can win games on technique alone. There is not going to be anybody that you play who is physically just going to grab you, shake you, throw you, and then go make a play. It cannot happen 80 times in a game. If you have breakdowns, it is going to be because somewhere along the line you had a technique error. It could be your first step, your aiming point, your strike position, if you had leverage, or whether you ran your feet or not. Something we really preach on is technique. Now, you can get up here and diagram plays and how you are going to stop plays. Schemes can be great. But it comes down to the technique and the execution of that technique that allows you to have success or not.

The third thing is that we have to play with intensity. It goes back to the attitude part. No other position on this football field hits somebody every snap. A guy on defense is trying not to get hit so he can make a play. A wide receiver is trying not to get hit, hopefully, so he can score. The quarterback does not want to get hit. You cannot allow that guy to get hit. The only position on the football field who hits somebody every play, or they are not doing their job, are the guys up front.

The fourth thing is, we want to make sure we compete. We must compete every down to win. I've got a young son who is 11. As he started to grow up he was playing T-ball and soccer and all of those youth sports. In the places where we lived, the younger you were, they never kept score. It drove me nuts that they couldn't keep score. In this life you either win or you lose. Not everyone can win, someone has to lose. You either win or you lose. Even though you might have won, you might not have given everything you had. Or even though you lost, you might have played the best you could play. But it is a team concept and you have to compete to be the very best you can all of the time. That is what we need to do.

The one thing we will get on our players about more than anything else is the lack of effort in terms of competing and competing to be the very best. I haven't had All-Americans to work with. One thing as an offensive line coach you will find is that you must have kids who are willing to overachieve. They must be better than what they are really capable of being. A lot of that is just how competitive that kid is and how competitive you make your environment. The overachievers are the guys who win games. Those are the musts that we as an offensive line need to adhere to.

We try to make it as simple for our front five guys as we can, both run and pass. In terms of breaking it down, we only want to be good at a few things. We want be good at five good things on running the football and five great things on throwing the football. You put those two things together and form fists and now you can go to battle.

When we want to run the ball it all starts with STANCE. It all begins and ends with a great stance. The second most important things are our STEPS. What is our footwork doing? The third is our STRIKE. We want to know how are we going to be able to deliver a blow on the defender and control the defender using our upper body and our hands.

The fourth one is the DRIVE part of it. How fast can we run our feet? The fifth thing is the FINISH.

Real quickly I will go through stance. Everybody has different ways of teaching a stance. But, again we are 50-50 so our stance has to be pretty balanced. When we talk about a stance, we want this, with the exception of the center. With the center the only thing different is that his feet are parallel and not staggered. We want a good solid base with the feet slightly wider than shoulders' width apart. We want a toe-to-instep relationship in terms of a stagger. So we have good flex in our ankles, our knees, and our hips. Again, we want our steps to be balanced. So when we go down, we want to be balanced on all three points of our body, and our fingertips, on the balls of our feet. So if I was looking to the side, I want all of our players to be balanced with a toe-to-instep relationship. Now again, you've got taller kids with longer cut legs, you have to give them a little bit bigger stagger, probably just a little bit wider in their base. We want their backs flat and their eyes up. We try to talk to them all the time in terms of "you cannot block what you cannot see." So it is important for them to be able to get a presnap look of the entire defense and what it is doing.

Now the determination of whether it is a run or if it is a pass comes into play. When it is a run, we talk to our players about slightly rocking forward and just mentally transferring all of the weight forward. So now they can be in more of a run mode. Their stance hasn't changed all that much. I may be in a slight rock or maybe a quarter of an inch. But I mentally transferred all of the weight. If it is a pass, we are going to slightly rock back. The difference between run and pass is not that noticeable for those people on the sidelines, or for the defensive guys on the other side of the ball. We try to talk to them all the time about this. We say, "Defensive players are dumb, but they're not stupid. They will read your stance. So try to disguise it as much as you can." Now again, do you get that all the time? No you don't, but it comes down to this: If you are going to give it away, whether it is a run or a pass, then you are telling me you are better than that guy. There is nothing that guy can do that you are not going to beat him, and not just beat him, but really physically and emotionally beat him. We don't spend a tremendous amount of time on stance, because everybody has to get into one that is comfortable.

Our steps are very important. Our first step as a center is no bigger than three inches. Our initial first step is no bigger than three inches. That is because I've got a nose usually sitting right on my face. For guards, tackles, and tight ends, their first step should be no bigger than six inches. That is a short six-inch step to the ball of my foot. That maintains that I can always have great power angles in my ankles, my knees, and in my hips. The common problem is that kids want to overstride or they want to overstep. The natural reaction is to step to their heels. If you step to your heel, your next movement is straight up, instead of coming out at a 45-degree angle.

The other thing we talk to our players about is that the first step is important and we have to get it on the ground. But, the most important step in terms of blocking, is the second step. That is when contact will be made. So your first step is important in terms of getting it on the ground whether it is three or six inches. It is important in landing on the balls of your feet and getting ready to have good power angles in your ankles, knees, and hips so you can explode off the ball. The second step is the one that you are actually going to drive with. So it has to be a short three- to six-inch step to the ball of your foot so you can maintain and keep all of your weight underneath you. Now the power angles in your ankles, knees, and hips can work together in terms of having an explosive nature off the ball.

When we go to strike we tell all of the offensive linemen, "God gave you these hands and arms to be great offensive linemen." The greatest thing that football could have done was allow offensive linemen to use their hands. Everybody is going to say, "All they do is hold." That is not holding to us, it is survival. It becomes survival, but it is a game of leverage and it is a game of pad control.

Now, in most conferences in college, and I don't know about in high school, but if you can strike within the framework of his body underneath the lips of his pads, regardless of what you do with your fingertips, you are good to go. It is that guy's fault on defense who allowed you to get in there. So we work on a lot of fast hand drills to try to get our hands in place inside. When we go to strike we are not windup guys. We don't wind up to go strike a blow. The reason I don't like to do this, after doing a lot of research, is this: One, it exposes your chest, and two, it raises your body up. So what we do is work on fast hands. We want to strike them straight from our stance, out. By throwing our hands out, what that will naturally force you to do, just to maintain your balance, is to get your first and second steps on the ground. If you don't move your feet you are going to fall flat on your face. You can't overstride by throwing your hands out. It is like a sprinter coming out of the blocks. He comes out and throws his hands and there is no way he can overstride. He has to get his feet on the ground so he can continue to run, then his arm action gets involved.

When we strike a blow, run or pass, it is always the same. It is with our thumbs up and our elbows in. The natural power line in your body, biomechanically, goes through your thumb, elbows, shoulders, lats, hips, knees, ankles, and to your feet. It is the natural power line of your body. It is a game of leverage. We try to control leverage.

The drive part is the next phase. We talk about driving all of the time. What we really want is for our kids to run their feet. In the old days the coach had you out there duck walking and doing other crazy things. They had you run "get-offs" in your stance and starts. All of a sudden he would have his kids come out of their stance and then chop their feet. You look at the Olympics. You don't see anybody run the 100-meter dash with their feet that wide apart. They can't run like that. So we talk about doing this. If you can strike a blow, get great leverage and great pad control on the defender, now it is up to you to run your feet. Use your speed to be able to maintain the block, or use your speed in terms of finishing the block. So instead of always harping on maintaining a good, wide base after contact, we talk in terms of just running your feet. Get going in a certain direction, the faster the better.

The next part about it is the finish. We talk about finishing all of the time. Call them pancakes, or call them whatever you want to call them. They are probably one of the four great feelings in life that any of us can ever have. Flat-backing a guy is one of them. The other three are up to your imagination. When you are able to put a guy on the ground, or on his back, that allows you, mentally, to establish physical domination. The thing that we try to talk about doing is this. If I am worth my salt as a defender, and a blocker is into me, and if I am halfway good, at some point in time I have to react to the ball. As that ball carrier comes, I have to try to take the pressure off the man to make the play. Once I release the pressure, that is when my feet continue to accelerate and I want to run through the block. That is when the decleaters or the pancakes happen. We talk about finishing all of the time. Finish the play you started.

Pass wise, we've got basically the same five components. One, it all starts with a great stance. Don't give it away. Don't give away your run and pass stance. Try to make it as close to the same as you can so you do not have to take any false steps.

Two, how fast and how strong are our sets? Three, what is our strike like? How do we strike a blow on our defender? Again, we want to make sure that we have pad control. Every defensive guy in America, if he has a choice to run through you or around you, he is going to run around you. So, if we get our hands on you, we feel like we've got an opportunity to win.

Number 4 is shuffling. There is a right way and a wrong way to shuffle. We want to make sure when we shuffle that we have all of our weight up and underneath us and not out to the sides. We want to be able to change direction when they change direction.

The last part is the finish. We will finish on throws as well. We don't cut. We want to make it at one point in time when you decide it comes back to a bull-rush situation, and now we can come back and finish you. When you are trying to bat the ball down, we are going to finish you. If you try to make it just a bull rush, then we are now going to try to make a run block. We want to try to get you back to the line of scrimmage to give the quarterback more of a cushion to throw. So we will put the physical part of the game back into protecting the passer.

Those are the five basic components. We already talked about the stance. We have three basic sets that we work on all of the time. It doesn't matter whether it is a Three-Step Drop or a Five-Step Drop, it is the same. We are going to set as tight to the line of scrimmage as possible. We are going to go on and do battle in this area. This is our battleground. If you happen to beat me, then that means you have to have great closing speed to get to the quarterback. This is as opposed to retreating and giving ground grudgingly. I have never seen someone give ground grudgingly. Not when you are trying to back up and he's running straight ahead. So we are going to try to do our battle as close to the line of scrimmage as possible. If you beat us, at least the quarterback has an opportunity to move.

We have three basic sets. One is a snap set, which means we are going to set on the line of scrimmage, or as tight to the line of scrimmage as we can. We have a wide outside set for any wide outside rushers. And we have a change of pace for what we call up-kick, which means we are going to change our set point. It could be on the line of scrimmage or wide and outside. We are going to be more aggressive and go get you, just to change our set points. We also up-kick on a lot of screens, which means we are going to get into you, and then we get rid of you, then we go.

What I want to talk about is the snap set first. When we snap set, the first and most important thing in terms of protecting the passer is getting out of our stance. We must be able to put speed back into the game. Again, the defensive line is using the ball as the trigger. We know the snap count, so everything is equal. But now we are trying to make it a foot race. He is running forward and I am running backward. Who is going to win? Unless I can physically get in front of the guy, he is going to win.

So when we snap set we try to do this. First, it all starts with a good, comfortable stance. My weight is evenly distributed. A pass has been called, so I am going to rock back. I mentally transfer the weight. From that point, I want to be able to get my head back as fast and as violently as possible. As I get into my stance, the first thing I want to concentrate on is snapping my head back as hard and as fast as I can. What that naturally does, even without using any hands, is it sinks my butt down so I have great power angles in my ankles, knees, and hips. I have the weight up and underneath me. It keeps my head back from trying to get overaggressive on the defender.

The first thing in terms of snap set is head back. The second thing is hands up. I'm going to throw my hands up as tight to my body as I can. The thumbs are up and the elbows in. I want them as tight to my body as I can. Reason being is this: Jerseys are getting tighter, and some are tighter than others. There are very few kids on defense who are now getting used to grabbing cloth and using it. What are they aiming for now? They're aiming for hands. They are trying to do all of the things the NFL guys do in terms of hand fighting and then being able to throw a move. We want our hands as tight to our body because basically we want to invite you to us. We want you to come and try to grab cloth and expose your chest. We want you to come and try to swat our hands. That means you have to close that distance that much more. So we want you to come to us. If they do not come to us, we just mirror them. If they want to play the game they will come to us.

We want the head back, hands up, and our hips will naturally fall back underneath us. We want to always maintain that our feet are buzzing. It is not chopping them up and down, it is just keeping them active. It is easier to move when they are moving than when they are stationary.

When we strike a blow, our guards and tackles will always try to strike inside hand first. The reason is because eventually he will have to close to me. He is a B-Gap rusher. He is either going to try to reach out and grab cloth or come straight through to me and bull rush me, or he is going to try to swat my hands. In any case he is going to expose himself. As I set, my feet are buzzing. I want to keep my outside hand as tight to my body as I can. I invite him to come that way. Then I am going to put my inside hand on him, thumbs up, elbows in, right under the lips of his pads, immediately followed by my outside hand. So it may look like we are trying to put them both on them at the same time, when in actuality we are trying to get our inside hand on him first. We want contact on the defender. So instead of one, now there is a second one. Bang! It is going to be done very, very quickly. Now all of the pressure goes with my outside hand. I can keep a great relationship with my outside eye with his inside eye and force him to make the next move. So we want to make sure that we strike with our inside hand first. For our tackles, it is really important. Now our jerseys are going to be real, real tight. We are going to keep that outside hand in and invite them to close that cushion on us and get as tight to us as they can. Now we have them. The thing we talk to our players about is this: You can fight your man in a lecture hall, and if you catch him there is a great chance you are going to beat the dog out of him. But you are expending a lot of energy just trying to catch him. Or you can fight him in a phone booth. If he comes to your body, you can get him into that phone booth. That is where you want to do battle. Again, most defenders will try to run around you rather than run through you.

With our centers, the thing we always try to get them to do is this: We talk in terms of having a stab hand. Our stab hand is nothing but the hand without the ball. What we try to teach our centers is not only to settle back and off the ball, but to snap set. So every time they set, they are going to settle back off the ball so they can get on the same plane as the guards. When that ball moves, that off hand is up. So simultaneously, that ball is the same direction. Ball back, hand up, and protect yourself. You are at a disadvantage anyway. One, you have a guy sitting right in your face mask. Two, you have to get a little bit of separation so you can get on the same plane as the guards. Three, you better get your off hand and stab hand on him to try to neutralize the guy in order to get your other hand up. Now you are like the rest of the guys. When that ball just starts to come back, that hand must be out. They are the only ones who can literally lock their arms out on a defender.

On the shuffle part of it we have two different shuffles. We always talk about shuffling the trail leg first. The first step I want to take is with my backside foot or my trail leg first. Reason being is if I step with my lead leg first, my weight is out to the side. It is no longer up underneath me. When that guy moves, I end up ripping out my groin trying to adjust to him. I want to make sure that by shuffling the trail leg first that I have my weight up and underneath me. I can transfer the weight, I can shuffle back and forth and basically mirror the guy.

When working in terms of shuffle, we break it down from strike to shuffle. We tell them the hands lock you on the block, but your feet do all of the work. The feet do all the work. This game is played from the waist down and it is important that your players understand that. I have seen a lot of players who could bench 500 pounds who couldn't play dead. That is because they don't know how to use their legs.

When we vertically shuffle, it is the same set as when we are outside. If I have a defender wide, a lot of people teach a kick step. That is the same thing that has just taken place when you shuffle lead leg first. What ends up happening when you kick step is your second step ends up coming to flat. Or, it ends up coming too deep. So on your third step you will end up dropping it to your own goal line, which creates a natural pass-rush lane, or shortens the corner for that defensive end. We are going to set with our inside foot. We are trying to get depth on our first step, and width with our second step. For an offensive tackle the best thing you can ever have is to have a guy on the outside shade such as a 5 technique, 6 technique, whatever you call it. Now you are in that box. I can get my hands on you and I can physically beat you.

My only chance is to get to that junction point where contact can be made. Then I can get my hands on you and we can go ahead and work it. It all starts with the set. Again, I'm going to stay heavy on my inside leg. I get depth and width. Now I am basically on my second step, which is the original position I was in my stance. If he is a little wider, inside out, I still have my weight underneath me. All of my weight is on my inside leg, so if he does want to come back inside, I still have a great strong post foot.

When contact is made, they have to keep the pass rushers on the line of scrimmage so the quarterback has someplace to go. The tackles have to be the athletes. They are responsible for the width of the pocket. They are naturally going to create throwing lanes if you can widen the guy. When contact is made, he is talking about being a C Gap or outside rusher. He is the contained rusher. He is always going to stay outside. So, if I can widen him by working the vertical, I am forcing him that much farther away from the quarterback. As opposed to this, I drop my foot to my own goal line and I turn and open. Now, I have done nothing to that throwing lane. I have created nowhere for that quarterback to go but up. We term that "working the vertical." The shoulders are square, outside hand in, and I am going to strike with my inside hand, trail leg first, trying to get depth and width on my footwork. I can always maintain that original position that I was in my stance.

Let me move to pass rush moves that defenders have. Again, the guys who you are going to play aren't going to use them all. They may not even use some of them. But, if you understand how many there are, and you have an answer for it before it ever arises, you look like you know what you are doing. That is the thing as coaches that we are trying to get people to do.

The thing that we talk about is this: A defense has only about four pass-rush moves. They have a bull or power rush, and a swim move. He has the move of the '90s, which is the speed rip. Then they have a spin move. We tell our guys even though there are only four moves, how many are they going to be good at? You can't be good at all four moves. You are going to be a mediocre player, because it is a game of reaction. So they are probably only going to be good off two of them. Each of those moves all work off each other. If you are a bull rusher, you can swim or spin or rip. You can rip and spin, but it is real difficult to rip and swim, or to rip and bull. You can't swim and spin or you just end up spinning yourself into the ground. So they all kind of balance out and work together. We try to talk about each of those moves and which ones they can be good at.

We only give our guys five days to think. They can think about the scheme, but they have to get to the point where they can react to the move. It is a game of reaction. Just like a golfer, it is the same being a pass protector. A lot goes into that swing. There are a lot of things that can go wrong, but the great ones are the ones who make it a natural reaction. It is the same thing in terms of pass protection. If you are thinking about it, then you are not going to be able to get it done. You have to be able to react to each of the moves that he throws a second ago in order to get your body into position to go out and get it done.

They are not very difficult to stop, but it is a reaction that you have to get your kids to do. I'm a firm believer in reps. We are very, very repetitive. We are creatures of habit. We do everything in our lives the same. When I talk about being creatures of habit, I tell the line this: What is the first thing you do when you wake up in the morning? I go to the bathroom, that is the first thing. It doesn't matter if you're 15 or 55, that is the first thing you do. You have trained your body to do that. You have trained your mind and body to react to the same thing at the same time. It is the same with being a good pass protector and good run blocker. You have to train your mind and body to react to the same thing at the same time.

Move-wise, it is four basic moves we use to stop them. The thing you have to remember is this. It is not all that difficult to stop them, but the thing you must get your kids to do is to react. The first thing we work on is a gunfighter drill. Which means we will get two kids to stand chest to chest, basically, hands down. All that we will do is, as fast as we can, once he sees movement he is going to try to put his hands on his chest. So it is really fast. We really work on shooting our hands inside. Once we get our hands inside, we are going to work on clinching. We want to be able to grab that plastic. We try to work on getting our hands inside as fast as we can. This will cause your kid's fingers to be sore, but they have to get used to it because they will be hitting someone every single time.

Now the bull rusher. Remember I talked about snap set, head back, butt down, and my hands up and inside. I want to keep them as tight to my body as I can. What he has to make sure that he does, is he is going to try to get his hands inside on me. If he sees my hands inside, where are his hands going to go? They will go out. If he sees my hands outside, where are they going to go? They will go inside. So, if I can keep my hands tight to the body, as he starts to come, I want to make sure that I can strike right under the lips of those pads and get a piece of that plastic. As he continues to try to bull-rush me, it means he's just going to try to walk me straight back to the quarterback. What I want to make sure that I can do is to get his chest, regardless of his height, in the air. It is that little V that comes down where his shoulder pads tie together. We talk in terms of shoving that thing into the guy's throat. It never happens, but it sounds good. We are going to try to shove his chest in the air to get him up. If we can get him up, and again it is a game of leverage, if I can get his chest in the air, regardless of whether I get that V in his throat or not, I can win. When I strike up, my hips will naturally sink down and he no longer has any forward thrust. So, the best way to stop a bull rusher is to get his chest in the air. Then, get ready to counter any move he has.

The next move is the swim move. Again, they're going to reach out and grab cloth or they will try to grab the triceps and turn your body. They try to get you to go someplace that he is not going. The one thing that is important to tell your kids is this. A short swimmer is not going to try to swim a tall guy. We talk in terms of pressure. Whether he is trying to grab, or swat, you fight that pressure. Remember, your hands are inside tight. They are still slightly bent at the elbows. When you feel it, you lock it out. You may not get it locked out, but you have started to straighten his body back out. So, when you feel pressure, you fight pressure. Now, as he either tries to come over the top or punch through, there is a major body part that is exposed and that is his lats. We want to get that open palm and jam it into his ribs as physically hard as we possibly can. Another term, we want to try to sauce a rib.

Once your hands are locked up, your feet have to do all of the work. Again, it is not real difficult, but it is training your mind and body to react to the same thing at the same time.

The third move is the move of the '90s, the rip move. Speed guys love the rip. Tall guys, short guys, everybody can rip. Basically what they are going to try to do is to try to get under you and create a mismatch in terms of speed. You are running backward, I am running forward. I am going to try to create a mismatch. My only hope is not to run through your body. You hear defensive line guys talk all of the time about working one half of the man. Don't work the whole man, but work one half of the man. So, as he tries to come through on that rip, he is going to rip that thing through and try to get his momentum to get vertically up the field. Then he is going to teach the rusher about leaning into him and running the hoops and trying to get back to the quarterback.

We have two thoughts where that happens. When they first started throwing the rip move, the original way of trying to stop it was this. As soon as he ripped it, coaches talked about keeping the arm locked out straight. Get your inside hand and put it to his hip. The thing that you ended up having was a lot of kids who couldn't physically change the pass rush by going to the hip hard. Or, as he continued to run up the field and he went to the hip, all he did was basically help him by. I got tired of being called for holding because my arms are on his neck. If you are not going to allow us to do this, then why don't you outlaw the move? They are not going to do that. So, what we will do when we have the rip guys is this. It is called clamping a guy. If the opponent is coming on me and contact is made, he is going to rip me half a man. What he is trying to do is to force my elbow up high so he can continue to run through me.

His coach has told him to make this fat guy work his feet. But what does the offensive line coach tell him? "You are not fat, you are an athlete." There are skilled guys, and there are athletes. Have you ever seen a skilled guy block an athlete? It can't be done. Have you ever seen an athlete try to catch a ball? It can't be done. There are skilled guys and there are athletic guys. That is us; we are the athletic guys. We don't want to work our feet. We want to get this guy in a phone booth. So, as he rips through, instead of going to the hip I am going to get his elbow and I am going to clamp it as hard to my ribs and my hip as I can. That forces him to play back into my body. Is it holding? No! Why? He got himself in that position, I didn't. We will clamp it so he has to work his little body into my big body. If I do not clamp hard, he will continue to rip it up. So we work on this drill all of the time. We are both standing up and we have him sprint up the field. He has to clamp him, and then shuffle vertically. We talk about the clamp all of the time. Now, where does our off hand go? Same place as it would if he was trying to swim me. I don't want to go low, because if I go low, my elbow will go up. I don't want it to go high, because now my elbow will go down, and he has my shoulder. It has to be right in the middle of his back, and what I want to do is to squeeze him and force him back to my body.

The last move is the Spin. They can come off a bull rush or, they can be off a rip, but they are all basically the same. A good spin guy is going to reach out, grab, and take the extra step, plant, accelerate, and try to get that fist with momentum to get himself vertically up the field. Whatever he hits along the way, that is great. The guys who don't try to build momentum, like a discus thrower or shot-putter who tries to block out, they are the ones who never go anywhere. They just stay in the same place going around in circles. If he gets a good clamp on me, it is real hard for me to try to pull that clamp out of there. Eventually I do have to let go, and I will, but initially for him to try to gain speed and momentum, it is tough. If he is loose with it, and he does pull off, remember, he has to release all of the pressure off you in order to spin. So when he releases the pressure off, you want to push and settle back inside.

We tell our line the defense will never spin away from the quarterback. If they do, let them go. Just turn them loose, because they are stupid. They will always spin to the quarterback. So, if I am a right tackle, he is only going to spin inside. If he goes away from the quarterback, let him go. The quarterback still has someplace to move. Center, you are in a bind because you are right in the middle. They only spin away. You always want to push and settle back inside. The key thing is this: You don't want to settle out early. You want to be able to push and settle.

Those are the moves we use. We talk to our kids in terms of this. Each one of those moves will always revert back to the same move, which is the bull rush. They revert back to it.

Chapter 15

ZONE BLOCKING CONCEPTS

By
Dan Young
University of Nebraska
1994

I am going to talk about techniques that we use at Nebraska and give you the Zone Package we use. At Nebraska we have two Offensive Line Coaches—Coach Milt Tenopir and myself. I work with the kickers, centers, and special teams. During that time Milt is down working with the tackles and guards. On other days Milt has the tight ends and tackles. When I bring my group down to join his group, I will take the tackles and he will take the guards and centers on combination blocks. Then we do individual blocking with the centers, guards, and tackles. Generally, I work on the Pass blocking and Milt handles the Run blocking.

When we have just the linemen we work against different fronts. I will take the Pass phase and Milt takes the Run part. We usually have a One and a Two Group and then we switch around. That is how we get prepared. When we come up to the field we have a kicking period. Then we have about three Team Stations. We have an Option, Run, and a Pass Station. This is all team work. That is how we split things up at Nebraska.

We grade each play after the games. In Spring Practice we grade every scrimmage. We scrimmage on Wednesday and Saturday. The way we grade our plays is this. If they go to the right spot, and do the right thing, and make the right block, they get a 2. If they go to the right place but do not do the right thing they get a 1. If they go the wrong way or screw up their block they get a zero. That is our grading system. We hope our players can get efficient enough to grade out to about 1.9. That is about 95 percent efficiency. You must have players that know what they are doing and they have to be dedicated and unselfish. They are not going to get a lot of glory. One of the reasons we like to run the football is because it highlights our offensive linemen. We can look at the stats and see where we stand as compared with other teams in the NCAA. They take a lot of pride in our standings in running the ball.

Since I work in the Passing Game we take a lot of pride in the low number of sacks we give up. The pro coaches tell me that if they can only give up five percent sacks they feel they are efficient. In the last year our line gave up six sacks in 220 passes. That comes out to about 2.65 percent. That means we did a good job protecting the passer. It is a little easier to protect our quarterback because a lot of our passes are Play-Action versus the Drop-Back Pass.

The first thing our players get after the game is their grade. Next they get the average grade for the entire team. We tell them if they can get close to a 1.9 average they have done well as a unit. The first thing we look at is Perfect Plays. To us, that is where all five linemen grade a 2 on the play. We like to have our players in the 65 to 70 percent category there. We look at Knockdowns, or Pancakes, and the number of times we put people flat on their back. Our goal as a team is to get 100 Knockdowns. We want our Offensive Line to get between 50 and 60 Knockdowns. It shows we are aggressive if we have a lot of Knockdowns. When you go against good teams it is hard to get Knockdowns. Against UCLA we had 24, and against Florida State we had 34. The better the teams, the more difficult it is to get Knockdowns. We still set a high goal and strive to get our average.

Next we look at Penalties. These are penalties that are caused by offensive linemen. We try to get that down to zero. Only in one game did we have zero penalties on the offensive line. Against Florida State we had two offensive penalties. These are the things we look at as offensive line coaches.

This is how we break down our offense at Nebraska. Run Plays are like the Toss Sweep, Draws, Fullback Traps, and those kinds of plays. You can see that was about 50 percent of our offense. Options were about 20 percent of our offense. Passes-Runs are plays where the quarterback ran the Bootleg or had to scramble on the play. Our quarterback is a good runner and he made a lot of yards on plays where pass plays were called. You can see our passing game was effective with over 51 percent completion.

PLAYS	ATT.	YDS.	AVE.
RUNS	441	2244	5.21
OPTIONS	141	410	6.45
PASS/RUN	37	164	4.40
TOTAL	619	3373	5.45
AVE.	51	281	40 TDs

PASSING ATTS. = 226 - 116 - 8
YARDS   51%   1711   7.57
AVE.   18   142   17 TDs
OFF. LINE - SACKS = 6 = 7.65

In the Orange Bowl we had a high percentage of third-down conversions. One reason for that is because of the type of offense we run. We keep the defense off balance. On third and long we are going to run the ball as much as we are going to throw the ball. You can see we run the ball about half of the time. The actual passes and the called passes are about 30 percent of the time. This will give you an idea where we are coming from when we talk about our offense.

This is our Zone Offensive Package. We went to this in 1991. We wanted to develop a blocking concept we could use for a number of different plays. We did not want a different blocking scheme for every play. We wanted to cut down on the amount of time Milt and I were spending trying to scheme plays rather than teaching players their techniques. We talked to the Bengals and Chiefs and watched a lot of film. We came up with something on our own as well. We went to this three years ago. We have won the Big Eight the last three years. It has been a good package for us.

Most teams today will put their best players on defense. I know when we sign a defensive tackle and he gets to us in fall practice and we find out that he runs a 5.4 for 40 yards, Coach Osborne meets him about halfway coming back to tell him he is now a member of the offensive line. Those are the kinds of players that end up on offense. They do not have the size and speed to play defense. This year we played with two tight ends. One was a converted wingback, and the other one was a walk-on. They ended up being good players for us. The point is this, our best outside linebackers are rush ends, but they could also be tight ends. However, we put our best players on defense to make things happen for us. It is not as easy to block those types as it used to be. That is another reason we went to the zone concept.

We run four different plays from the Inside Zone Concept. We run our Dive, Give-to-the-Fullback off our pitch action. Then we run the Give-to-the-Fullback off our Dive Option action. Then we run our One-Back Dive from the One-Back Set, which is a Zone Read. It is from the I-Back Set where he cuts it back or stays onside. The other play is a Two-Back Draw where we can run it to the tight-end side or the split-end side. When we run to the tight-end side we have two different ways to run the Draw.

We run four different plays from the Outside Zone Concept. We run the Toss Sweep, a One-Back Outside Dive, a pure Outside Option off our Dive Option action, and our Speed Option out of our One-Back Set. Those four plays are all packaged off our Outside Zone Concept.

Then we have Misdirection plays. We run our Dive Pass where the quarterback comes out naked, and a Draw Pass where it looks like Zone Action and we pull the uncovered lineman out to the back side. We also have a little Shovel Pass where we bring the Wingback around back underneath off our Dive one way. Then we run our Tackle Trap where we look like we are running Dive one way, but it is a designated cutback. We trap with the Tackle either on the linebacker or the 2 technique depending on the kind of look we face. This is what I would like to go over with you today.

This is what our Zone Offensive Package looks like. Hopefully, you will be able to see what we are trying to accomplish with our Zone Blocking Scheme.

INSIDE ZONE SERIES

A. Covered - Stretch Base

B. Uncovered - Stretch Double

C. 33-37 Dive, FB Give from Pitch Action

D. 11-19 Dive, FB Give from Dive-Option Action

E. 43-47 Dive, 1 Back Dive

F. 43-47 Draw, 2 Back FB Lead
       1. Open Side
       2. TE Side

OUTSIDE ZONE SERIES

A. Covered Rip-Reach

B. Uncovered Pull and Over Take

C. 41-49 Pitch, Toss Sweep
   1. Open Side
   2. Tight Side

D. 41-49 Outside, One-Back Outside Dive
   1. Open Side
   2. TE Side

E. 11-19 Base Option, Dive Option Action
   1. Open Side
   2. TE Side

F. 31-39 Sprint Option, One-Back Sprint Option
   1. Open Side
   2. TE Side

MISDIRECTION

A. 43-47 Dive Pass. Dive Action naked Boot

B. 43-47 Draw Pass. The 2 Back Draw Action - Uncovered Lineman Lead

C. 43-47 Dive WB Shovel Pass

D. 43-47 Tackle Trap. Designated IB Cutback.

The reason we like the Zone Concept is because it is simple. We just tell our linemen they have to know two things, basically. They need to know if they are covered or uncovered. If you are covered and we run an Inside Zone, you do what we call a Stretch Base. If you are uncovered you come and help another blocker. We call that a Stretch Double. We are thinking double team where one of the two will come off late for the linebacker. If you are covered and the backside man is also covered, we know we have a Stretch Base, but we are not going to get any help. That is the play. That is all they have to know. When we get into the Draw, we have to know who the Fullback is blocking, so we have a small adjustment there. Basically, that is the concept we use; Covered or Uncovered.

If I am covered, the first thing I want to do is to take a Stretched Step. That is a quick lateral. We do not want to come upfield. It all depends where the defender is as to how big the step will be. If the defender is on the blocker, it will be a simple change of weight on the feet. We used to step, and the defense would step to the side and we ended up with no leverage. We want to get our belly upfield. We want to keep our heels pointed toward the goal line as long as we can. So, the first step is all determined by where the defender is aligned. If he is wider I will take a longer Stretch. It will be a quick lateral step. The second step is right in the middle of his cylinder. We step without crossing over. The young players tend to cross over and then lose their base. The second step is in the middle. We bring up the hands in the middle of the defender's cylinder and start driving him. If we have help, we are eyeballing the linebacker all of the time this is happening. If you do not have help you stay with the defender all the way. It is a stretch step, second step to the middle, do not cross over, rip up. We try to invite movement. We do not care if they are running. That is fine. If they want to run, we will get back underneath them. We do not have to knock them on their backs and cut them off, and all of that. We invite movement and just run them. That is the Covered Principle.

If I am Uncovered this is what we do. We tell him to take a 45-degree step and aim for a point on the back of the hip of the defender. If he gets to the man and the hip is still there he stays with it. If the hip disappears he goes up to the linebacker. If he gets to the hip of the lineman he does not come off until he gets to the linebacker's depth. So often what happens is they want to come off the block too early. The most important thing is to get movement at the line. Sometimes we drive the lineman into the linebacker. You have to eyeball the linebacker to see what happens. We do not have to worry about who is going to block each man if they slant. We drill it over and over again and it becomes automatic for our linemen. You will see in our films teams that try to slant and play games against us just take themselves out of the play. We have good running backs at Nebraska and they can read the blocks up front. They can cut off the blocks. We just get the defense moving and take them the way they want to go.

The center has a tough block if the backside guard is covered. He knows he is not getting help from the backside guard, even though the nose is lined up six inches away. Sometimes we will have the center scramble block rather than take the man one on one with this Stretch Base Scheme. Since the center has to make quick contact we will overstretch the center at times to make sure we get penetration stopped. The thing that hurts the Inside Zone play more than anything else is penetration. If you can keep the defense at the line of scrimmage and get them running, the backs can find a place to run the ball.

If the guard is uncovered the backside tackle will check out. If the play is going away from him he will check down the line. If a man is there he run him down the line. If the man is stretched we run with him. If we can cut him off we will.

All of this looks easy but it takes a lot of time to perfect. That is why we have gone to this scheme because we feel we can spend more time working on technique. It takes a lot of repetitions. Our splits on the Outside Zone is tighter than on our Inside Zone. We split one foot on the Outside Zone and a foot and one half on the Inside Zone. If the split is big you have a bigger chance for penetration. The technique we use on our Outside Zone has to be tight.

We have two Fullback Give plays either off our Dive Option action or off our Pitch action. We used to run the pitch like Florida State and Auburn run it. We have hit so many 3 linebacker setups we had to change the way we run the pitch. When I get to the Outside Zone I will go over that. Our fullback aims a little wider than he did before on our Pitch Toss Sweep play. On our Dive Option action the fullback aims at the butt of the guard. The fullback comes off his butt and we read the onside crease. If the play is not open he is not going to cut until he gets up into the hole. We tell the back to get to heels' depth of the lineman before he cuts. We do not want them to start cutting back too soon. If people start playing the cutback too soon it will not work. The deeper you can get the back up in the hole, the better you will be. We tell them Smooth to the hole, and then Speed through the hole.

The defense we see more than any other is the offset 4-3 look. You can see the rules as they apply on our Dive Option vs. and even front.

DIVE OPTION VS. EVEN

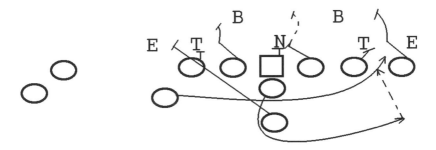

Look at the play against the odd front. Now the center has the nose by himself.

DIVE OPTION VS. ODD

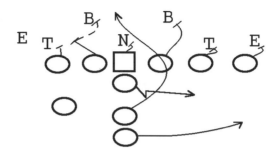

It is a simple concept of who is blocking who. The players cannot say they do not know who they are blocking. You get a body on a body. You do not have people unblocked. This has helped us a great deal.

The next play is the Lead Draw. This gives us an effective running play to the split side. On a 4-3 setup we want the fullback to block the outside linebacker to the onside. You do not have to use a different rule to the other side. You can have the same rule to the tight-end side and all you have to do is to have the tight end release to force. To the open side we bring the fullback on the outside linebacker. The onside guard and center work on the nose and middle linebacker.

LEAD DRAW OPEN SIDE VS. EVEN

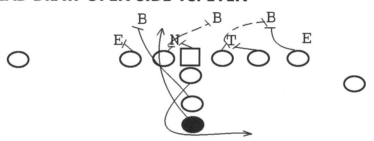

LEAD DRAW TO TE VS. ODD

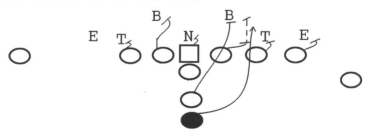

If we get a Split Six look we still get the fullback as an extra blocker on the linebacker. The tight end makes an out call. We end up coming over one man. Our fullback is 5 yards deep and the tailback is 8 yards deep on their alignment. The quarterback gives the back the ball as deep in the backfield as he can.

Next I want to go over what we do on the Outside Zone. Again, it is the same concept. It is covered or uncovered principle. If you are covered we say you are going to rip reach, and if you have backside help you are going to escape. If you are uncovered you are going to pull and overtake. That is all the linemen have to know; who is covered and who is uncovered. If I am covered and the play is going to my side then I am going to rip reach and escape to the linebacker. We are going to try to get the play outside with this scheme. We are running the Toss Sweep, the Outside Dive Option, the Speed Option, or the Pitch Outside. We are running our Outside Zone play. It is very similar blocking. The covered man takes a stretch, and then he crosses over and tries to get belly upfield. We want to rip with the hand when we get to the defender to help the other blocker pick him up. The split is only about one foot. We want the uncovered man to pick him up. The man that is pulling just keeps pulling but he must eye the linebacker. If the linebacker plays under he comes off and picks him up. If he doesn't come off, the puller will end up going around the man that is rip reaching.

ONE-MAN SET SWEEP VS. ODD

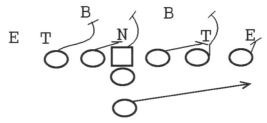

Let me give you the Two-Back Toss Sweep against the odd front. Now we have the fullback lead the play. We do run the play to both sides; tight end or open side.

TWO-BACK TOSS SWEEP VS. ODD

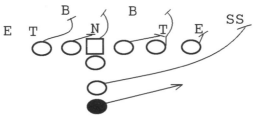

We used to run the Toss Sweep like Florida State runs it. When we played teams like Miami and Florida State the Sam linebacker would have a heyday. We could not run the play. We went to the Outside Zone Concept and it has helped us a great deal.

The next thing we look at is our Sprint and Dive Option action. Our rule is this. If we go to the split end side we are going to pitch off the end man. If we go to the tight-end side we are going to pitch off the force man.

OPTION - SPLIT SIDE

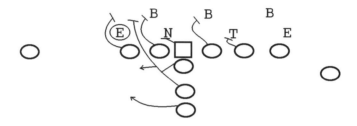

If we are running the Option to the tight-end side we pitch off the force man. This is a good play against third-down situations when teams are playing the pass. The One-Back Sprint Option was more effective than the Two-Back Option.

OPTION - TIGHT END SIDE

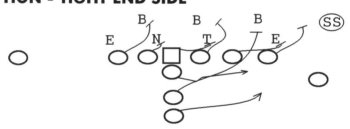

If we are going to run Dive Option action it is the same deal. We have the luxury of having the fullback to help on anyone that filters through our line.

Let me cover our Misdirection off our zone action. The plays include the Dive Passes, the Draw Passes, and the Tackle Trap, and the Wingback Shovel Pass. A lot of times we run our Dive Passes out of our Ace Formation where we keep our tight end in to block, and the quarterback is not completely naked. We give the line this rule on Naked: Everyone pulls one man to the call. If there is no one there, block the man on you. That is where the rule ends. One man to the called side. If the tackle is uncovered and the defense has two men outside, the tackle can give the guard a call and we will pull two men to the called side. They are the only two that would pull to the call. Normally we pull one man to the call. If you are covered, block the man on you. We try to make the play look like we are running the Inside Zone action. The quarterback goes naked away from the action. The end runs an 18-yard comeback route. The Pro Back runs a horn on the other side. Those are the two receivers the quarterback looks for.

NAKED BOOTLEG

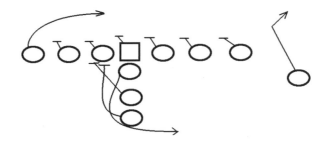

NAKED BOOTLEG VS. EVEN

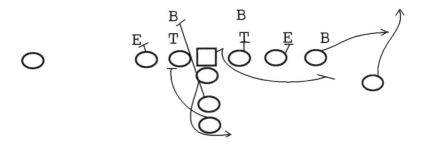

If we face an even look the center pulls. We can have a delay route with the tight end. The split end is coming across. We like to get a man out leading the quarterback.

Next is the Shovel Pass. We run it off the Dive. The fullback blocks to the side the wingback is lined up. The wingback and quarterback must read the defensive end. If the end drops off, the wingback may end up blocking him and the quarterback keeps the ball on a run. It is a simple play that has worked very well for us. We can run this play from the Shotgun Formation.

SHOVEL PASS

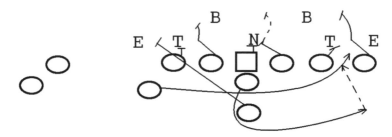

The last Misdirection we run is a designated cutback that we run where we trap with the tackle. We bring either the guard or center off on the linebacker. The I-back gets the ball about 3 yards from the line. He cuts it back underneath keying the block of the tackle. If we are going to the right we call the play 43 so it looks like we are running 43 Draw. It is a designated cutback for the I-back. When you get to running the Zone Play very effectively everyone starts running to the ball. If you have tackles that can pull like we have, they will love this play. We can trap the down lineman and let the end block the linebacker.

TACKLE TRAP

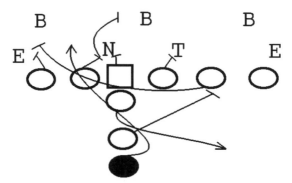

Those are our Misdirection plays off the Zone action.

About the Editor

Earl Browning, the editor of the By the Experts Series, is a native of Logan, West Virginia. He currently serves as president of Telecoach, Inc.—an organization that conducts football clinics and produces the Coach of the Year Football Manuals. A 1958 graduate of Marshall University, he earned his M.Ed. and Rank I from the University of Louisville. From 1958 to 1975 he coached football at various Louisville-area high schools. Among the honors he has been accorded are his appointments to the National Football Foundations and the College Hall of Fame Advisory Committee on moving the museum to South Bend, Indiana.